Study Less, Learn More

The Complete Guide for Busy Students

Michael W. Wiederman, PhD

ISBN-10: 0-9818534-1-2
ISBN-13: 978-0-9818534-1-3

Special thanks to my colleague

Kyle Love

for her encouragement

and valuable feedback in

the completion of this book.

Michael W. Wiederman, PhD

Contents

Michael W. Wiederman, PhD

Welcome

Congratulations on your decision to take a look at this book. Consistently, surveys have revealed that the large majority of students rely on study techniques that researchers have found to be among the least effective options. On the one hand, we shouldn't be surprised; formal education typically focuses on *what* to study, not *how* to study. The goal here is to remedy that in the most direct and least painful way.

It's important to point out that this book is based on what research by psychologists has revealed about learning and studying. The advice in these pages *doesn't* come from successful students or teachers, based on their experiences and beliefs. Instead, the advice is based on approaches tested and found effective using the scientific method.

Rather than making this a book about the research on learning and studying, it's a "how to" manual. Accordingly, I've tried to keep the book as pared down as possible, including only what I think is necessary to improve your studying (and perhaps to convince you to change your behavior). So, I resisted providing detailed descriptions of the research upon which the book is based (but there is a Reference Notes section at the end that cites the research, for those who want to delve deeper).

Also, everything described in this book is meant to work together as a coherent package. I had to write in separate chapters, simply because there is no possible way to communicate everything at once. However, no one technique or strategy is a miracle solution. Also, some concepts are introduced in one chapter and then tied to practical strategies in subsequent chapters. I say all of this to stress the importance of reading all of the chapters in order, and then integrating the pieces for maximum payoff.

I hope you find this book both easy to understand and remarkably useful. Regardless, I welcome all comments and suggestions: Michael@mindingthemind.com.

Cheers,

Michael Wiederman

For more tips, updates, and online videos, go to www.MindingtheMind.com/Studying.

Learning

Why are you studying? What are you hoping to get from all your work? It may seem like an obvious question, but an honest and accurate answer is important for determining how much you'll get from this book, or how you'll best use it.

The two most common goals for studying are 1) to understand the material and expand your permanent knowledge, skills, and abilities, and 2) to score highly on exams and eventually earn some sort of diploma. Of course completion of the first goal leads to completion of the second, but not the other way around. That's why it's important to be clear about your *true* goals.

How did there get to be two goals instead of just the first one? Of course the original and ultimate purpose of education was and is to expand permanent knowledge, skills, and abilities. However, exams and grades entered the scene to help motivate studying and to ensure that all successful students reach at least a pre-set minimum level of achievement in a particular course of study. Believe me, no one likes exams and grades, including teachers. Optimistic teachers still hope that students, at least at the upper levels of the formal educational system (such as high school and college), want to learn for the sake of understanding and personal growth. On the other hand, many teachers have grown discouraged and assume that students are only concerned with grades. Why might it seem this is often the case?

Because grades are much more concrete than "knowledge, skills, and abilities"—they're more immediate, clear, and definite—many students tend to slip into focusing on grades as the measure of whether they've done a good job learning. Good students earn good grades, right? So, if you earned a good grade, you must have done what was expected of you. You're done! Whew.

Now think back to exams you took, courses you completed, and good grades you earned for both. How much do you remember from those exams and courses? How well did the material become integrated into what you know, and how you think, and who you are?

Perhaps you are one of those relatively rare students who do indeed study with the genuine goal of long-term learning rather than short-term exam performance. If so, that's great! However, in the spirit of being honest with ourselves, I have to confess that I was the type of student I assume is the majority. For a total of 22 years I was a student formally enrolled in compulsory school, college, and graduate school. For virtually all of that time, my emphasis was on doing the least amount of studying to earn a good grade. How much I had "learned" or changed from the studying was of little concern. Knowing what I do now, I would have a much different focus as a student, and I hope to convince you that it's in your best interest to learn from my mistakes.

The good news is that studying for true knowledge and understanding does not take longer than studying simply to do well on exams, and it's certainly more engaging, meaningful, and long-lasting. The point of this book is to use what psychologists have discovered about learning and studying in the most efficient ways possible. By "efficient," I mean the least amount of time and effort for the greatest degree of long-term learning. This book isn't about "beating the system," but about gaining a true education without devoting every waking hour to school.

I wish I could offer some miracle method that involved very little effort with huge payoffs on test scores. If there was such a thing, I'd be thrilled to share it. In reality, anyone who makes such promises is lying. Psychologists have tested the various shortcuts touted over the years, including hypnosis, subliminal techniques, and exposure to information while asleep (none of which work), as well as various methods to develop "super memory" (which do work to some degree but require lots of practice).

There are no shortcuts to any place worth going.

— Beverly Sills

Let's be practical and ask, "Why should I study with the goal of deeper understanding and long-term knowledge?" Let's start with perhaps the most important practical reason: a network of established knowledge makes it easier to learn new information. Think of your fund of knowledge (what you "know") as a large mesh ball made of tangled wire, with each strand being a separate bit of knowledge. As long as we're using this mesh ball analogy, let's assume that where two bits of wire touch or cross, the knowledge they represent is somehow related.

Now, imagine trying to learn something new, or adding a bit of wire to the structure. The more you know, the easier it is to find a "hook" onto which this new bit of knowledge fits (is associated with something already there). If you knew nothing that could relate to this new bit of information, it's not likely to become a permanent part of your overall knowledge structure.

This principle that prior knowledge makes new knowledge easier to acquire explains why experts on a particular topic have an easy time integrating new information about their topic of expertise. They have a rich network of crisscrossing knowledge, and when they encounter something new, it's easy to see how the new bit fits into the bigger picture. That is, they better understand that aspect of the world. So, it's a case of the rich becoming richer (where the richness is in knowledge anyway).

Now let's consider a statement we've all said: "Why do I have to learn this? I'll never need it in real life!" It is true that much of the knowledge you're exposed to (and supposed to learn) will not be "used" directly at some future point. Still, think about the mesh ball analogy. All knowledge and learning builds onto your mental network. A "well-rounded" education means creating some mesh structure in lots of different areas so that when you encounter something (anything) in the future, you'll hopefully have some context for understanding it (and possibly using it). Knowledge is not simply a collection of facts, but an integrated web of deeper understanding and the ability to apply and adapt what you know.

Too often "education" is equated with "learning stuff," or accumulating information, but lasting education also involves *how to think.* In addition to knowing a lot, a smart person is good at learning, reading and writing, analyzing information, thinking logically and critically, articulating his or her thoughts, and so forth. These intellectual skills have to be learned and then practiced, just like any other skills.

When someone goes to the gym and lifts weights repetitiously in various ways, do we ask, "Why are you doing *that*? You'll never use those movements with those weights out in real life!" Instead, we recognize that the exercises will build stronger muscles, and that's the whole point. Well, much of school work is meant to build your intellectual "muscles," but the growth is not as visible as skeletal muscle. Think of each class meeting, homework assignment, and study session as working out your mind and intellect.

If you're going to spend your time and energy studying, do you want to get the most lasting benefits? Or, are you willing to lose out on the best of what is meant by being educated? In my case, I consistently racked up good grades, so I earned diplomas along the way. Unfortunately, I didn't learn very much despite all those years and lots of effort. My goal was always to finish the exam or assignment with a good grade, without much concern for deeper understanding or long-term retention. Will you make the same incredibly costly mistake?

Our modern era, often termed the Information Age, has never been called the Knowledge Age. Information does not translate directly into knowledge. It must first be processed—accessed, absorbed, comprehended, integrated, and retained.

-- Noted psychologist Robert Cialdini, in his book *Influence*

*Education is what survives when what
has been learned has been forgotten.*

-- Legendary psychologist B. F. Skinner

*The only person who is educated is the one who has
learned how to learn . . . and change.*

-- Legendary psychologist Carl Rogers

*The individual who is best prepared for any occupation
is the one whose intelligence has been so well trained
that he is able to adapt himself to any situation
and whose point of view has been so humanized
by his education that he will be a good person
in any job or calling.*

-- Mortimer Smith

*It's possible to store the mind with a million
facts and still be entirely uneducated.*

-- Alec Bourne

Beliefs

Psychologists have revealed a number of beliefs that affect how people perform academically. The sneaky part is that we're typically unaware of how our beliefs shape our learning, or perhaps even that we hold such particular beliefs.

Entity Theorists vs. Incremental Theorists

Think of the various kinds of intelligences or abilities people possess. These might include musical ability, mathematical ability, and verbal ability. Now, which of the following two statements most closely matches what you assume (believe) about these various forms of intelligence?

1) How intelligent you are (your abilities) in a particular area is generally a given, perhaps based on your genetic makeup or your earliest childhood experiences.

2) How intelligent you are (your abilities) in a particular area is generally the result of how much effort you put into learning and practicing in that area.

Of course, neither statement is entirely false or inaccurate, but do you lean in one direction in your view of why people vary in their intelligences? What about the types of intelligences most important for learning in school, such as math and language?

What's important for us here is whether holding one belief more than the other is related to learning. Psychologists have studied differences between people who tend to lean toward the first statement ("Entity Theorists" they call such people) and people who tend to lean toward the second ("Incremental Theorists"). I assume the labels come from the fact that statement #1 implies that intelligence is an entity that resides within the individual—it's something the person possesses and carries around with him- or herself. Statement #2 implies that intelligence is something that can be gained in increments through effort, and mostly comes down to how much the person wants to invest in mastering something.

Entity Theorists may reveal themselves through how they describe themselves and others: "Well, members of my family just aren't math people, so I was lucky to pass that math course." Or, "John got all the musical ability in our family; I can't carry a tune even if it has handles." Or, "I'm just not a good test taker." Incremental Theorists also may recognize that people seem to vary in how easily they learn particular skills compared to others. Still, the general belief is that anyone can excel in an area if that person invests enough time and effort.

As you might imagine, Incremental Theorists are more likely than Entity Theorists to persist in studying or working on something, even if it is difficult at first. It's not that Entity Theorists are lazy, but the importance of protecting self-esteem plays an important role. If we believe that our intellectual ability is inherently a part of us, and we put a lot of effort into studying, what does it mean if we should still do poorly?

That scenario might imply that we're not very intelligent after all. However, if we do not expend much effort, and we do poorly, we have a legitimate excuse. "My score doesn't reflect my underlying intelligence because I didn't fully apply myself." Incremental Theorists are less likely to fall prey to this self-esteem-protecting trap because, if they do poorly, they assume they can do better by simply studying more.

Unfortunately for Entity Theorists, the process of protecting self-esteem is an unconscious one. So, it's easy to assume this trap doesn't apply to us, even if we admit to being Entity Theorists. Rather than remain in denial, the best thing to do is simply work on becoming more of an Incremental Theorist.

Spend some time thinking through whether the Incremental Theory seems accurate to you. If learning something in particular doesn't come easily for you, do you think you *could* master it if you had a large enough incentive and spent considerable time and effort working on it? Simply being convinced that your ultimate success in learning depends mainly on your effort is the important thing to establish. How easy or difficult it is to learn something doesn't indicate your level of intelligence or worth.

Only the curious will learn and only the resolute
will overcome the obstacles to learning.
The quest quotient has always excited me
more than the intelligence quotient.

-- Eugene S. Wilson

Hello Hindsight Bias

There is another sneaky belief that causes trouble when learning. Unfortunately it's a natural result of the way our minds work. Psychologists have named it "hindsight bias" because this mental blind spot comes into play *after* we've learned something.

If we don't know something, and we're tested on it, we're aware of our ignorance ("I don't know that!"). However, once we've learned it, there is no way to go back and experience the same state of mind we had before we knew it. In other words, we can recognize intellectually that we had to learn the new material, but we can no longer *feel* what it was like to be ignorant of this material that we've now learned.

OK, so what? Well, this hindsight bias leads to overestimating how much we knew about the topic before the actual learning occurred. It seems that, now that we know something, it sort of feels "natural" to know it. It's now a given—no big deal. As a result, we also tend to overestimate the extent to which other people have the same level of knowledge

For students, hindsight bias often leads to not taking enough notes, or not including enough detail in their notes. As you read or hear something and it "makes sense," it's almost as though hindsight bias is whispering, "You know this now. You'll remember it." Of course that isn't always the case, and you may not even know that you've forgotten something because you don't have any mention of it in your notes. Or, your notes on the topic are so general and vague that they don't make sense later. At the time, though, you felt confident that the notes you made captured what you then "knew" (thank you hindsight bias!).

When studying, hindsight bias makes us feel too confident that we know something. If we review our notes or an assigned reading, we recognize the information, and hindsight bias leads us to feel that we actually *know* the material. Of course we'll tackle the issue of working around hindsight bias in the chapters on studying and taking notes.

The Curse of Expertise

Unfortunately, hindsight bias applies to teachers, too. In this case, though, it leads to overestimating the degree to which students have the same knowledge and ways of thinking about the material that the teacher takes for granted. Obviously, teachers recognize that students aren't at the same level of knowledge and expertise, but they do tend to overestimate what is "basic" in a particular field.

Because teachers know particular content and ways of thinking about their particular field very well, hindsight bias blinds them to what it was like to have been in the students' shoes. The results are often confused students and frustrated teachers. When applied in this way, psychologists refer to the phenomenon as "the curse of expertise." The curse is the assumption that knowledge familiar to the individual is "common knowledge" or "common sense" among others (especially students who "should have learned this already" in previous courses).

The curse of expertise shows itself when a teacher is presenting material to students and says, "Obviously, blah blah blah . . .," or "And of course, blah blah blah . . .," and the students are each thinking, "Obviously?! Of course?! I don't know what the heck is going on!" Or, what about when a teacher assigns work that requires background knowledge that most students actually do not have?

Sometimes a student *should* have learned something before now and hasn't (recall my own experience). However, if *most* students do not know something the teacher assumes they do, that sounds like a case of hindsight bias (the curse of expertise type).

I'll never forget an incident during my first week of graduate school. All of the brand new doctoral students in psychology had to take a two-semester sequence of statistics courses. To "assess where we were," our professor administered an exam over "basic material" we "should have learned as undergrads." We all bombed! We had all been successful college students with top grades and had been selected into this competitive doctoral program, yet we knew very little on this supposedly "basic" exam!

It was true that we all had statistics courses as undergraduates, but that fact was a far cry from having mastered particular statistical material and being able to use it "cold" two or three years later. How did the professor respond? With disappointment and rage, and he let us know all about it! Despite being a psychology professor, he assumed we were slackers rather than recognizing his own case of the curse of expertise.

Unfortunately, it's up to students to be familiar enough with the curse of expertise not to let it discourage them when it rears its head. Remember that teachers may very well be mentally blind to what their students do and do not know, and how their students think about the material. If a teacher seems to assume you know something, or know how to do something, but you don't, be sure to ask for some explanation or instruction.

Too often students believe that they must be the only ones who don't know this "assumed" material or way of doing something. Why? Because 1) the teacher is acting as though all students should know it, and 2) no other students are speaking up to question that assumption. Rather than be embarrassed that you are the only student who doesn't "get it," be the class hero who asked for the blanks to be filled in. Regardless of whether your classmates appreciate your courage, your own degree of learning (and your grade) will benefit.

Beliefs About Learning

There is a very simple yet troublesome belief many of us seem to hold, not really thinking about it consciously: The belief that learning shouldn't require a great deal of effort or time. This is probably especially true for Entity Theorists, who think, "If I'm smart, it shouldn't take much for me to know this."

We know from experience that there are times when we learn something quickly and easily, or even without any conscious effort at all. As a result, we may fall into assuming that learning is "naturally" or "normally" that way. This is a nice fantasy, but we'll see as we consider attention and memory in subsequent chapters, it's unrealistic unless the material to be learned is inherently interesting or engaging.

Expect learning assigned material to be effortful, and sometimes even frustrating. To expect otherwise is to set yourself up for failure. If learning was normally easy, everyone would be well-educated. Still, at least when you follow the advice in this book, studying will be anything but boring.

Learning Styles

The topic of learning styles has become so pervasive in our culture that people seem not to question it. The assumption is that people vary in the ways they best learn, so being able to match class instruction (or studying) with the individual student's learning style will result in the greatest learning (and the least frustration).

More than 30 years of research and writing on learning styles has resulted in thousands of articles and reports. Unfortunately, the bottom line is that there is no agreement on what types of learning styles exist or are important, how they can be measured accurately, or how learning styles should affect teaching and studying. Accordingly, decades of research has failed to consistently demonstrate that learning styles matter.

In a book on the 50 greatest myths of popular psychology, learning styles made the list. The authors ended the section on learning styles with this summary: "So, the popular belief that encouraging teachers to match their [teaching styles] to students' [learning styles] enhances their learning turns out to be an urban legend of educational psychology." Ouch.

Does it hurt to continue to believe that you should determine and then cater to your own learning style? Perhaps. Research has shown that using a greater range of different types of teaching approaches to cover the same material is most effective generally. So, limiting yourself to one strategy may not be wise. Also, not all material, or all settings outside of school, allow for adapting to your preferred style of learning. By focusing on one style, you further make yourself dependent on it as you fail to get practice at learning through a variety of methods.

That last point reminds me that people seem to take pride in their strengths while avoiding those areas in which they are weakest. This tendency makes sense as a way to protect our self-esteem. However, over time we becoming increasingly lopsided and limited. Instead, what about thinking of education as deliberately remedying our weaknesses? The goal is to end up more flexible and competent overall.

Let go of beliefs in learning styles and instead focus on applying the approaches research has demonstrated to be the most effective. Also, challenge yourself to work in ways that remedy your weaknesses rather than simply reinforcing your strengths.

Unless you try to do something beyond
what you have already mastered,
you will never grow.

-- Ronald E. Osborn

Attention

Learning starts with attention. If we don't focus on something there is no chance that it will become something we remember. Seems obvious, yet there seem to be some common misunderstandings about attention.

Psychologists make the important distinction between when things grab our attention ("bottom-up attention") and when we intentionally focus our attention ("top-down attention"). When we're intensely engaged in top-down attention, our focus might be so complete that we fail to notice other things going on around us. At other times, even though we're attempting top-down attention, bottom-up attention easily demands our focus.

Typically, top-down attention is effortful and bottom-up attention is not. Learning something that doesn't naturally hold our attention takes effort and mental resources. When something interests us (bottom-up attention), learning feels relatively effortless. This explains why we seem to naturally remember so much about topics that interest us and so little about topics we had to force ourselves to study (top-down attention).

Because top-down attention is required for deliberate learning, anything that detracts from top-down attention, or makes it more difficult, impairs learning. Unfortunately, this is the case with multitasking.

Multitasking

Many people think they can focus on more than one thing at a time, or "multitask," and perform as well as if they were focusing on only one of those things. Chances are that you're one of those people (don't worry; most people share your belief).

In reality, our attention or focus is like a spotlight, illuminating only what it's pointed on at the time. The "top-down" versus "bottom-up" labels simply refer to what is determining where the spotlight is pointed-- us or the environment. As our attention shifts, the spotlight is simply moved from one place to another, but it can only be focused in one place. If a spotlight cannot be focused on two places at once, why does it feel like we can effectively multitask, or do two things at once?

Psychologists have found that multitasking often involves rapidly shifting attention or focus between two or more tasks. That is, we are not technically doing two (or more) things at once (at exactly the same time), but rather are very quickly going back and forth between the tasks. Sometimes multitasking is absolutely necessary, but if it's not, we're better off focusing on one thing at a time, especially when learning.

One problem with multitasking is that it uses more of our mental reserves, depleting them sooner than concentrating on one thing. Also, the shift in attention or focus always involves a bit of lag, or catching up, with each act of shifting. Using the analogy of the spotlight, it takes a small bit of time and effort to aim the spotlight on exactly the right place again after having been focused elsewhere. So, divided attention is inefficient, and there is always the risk of missing something important while the spotlight is pointed elsewhere.

When we cover how memory works in a subsequent chapter, it will be clearer why learning suffers during multitasking. In the meantime, think about when you study or do homework. Do you focus on only one thing at a time? What about music, television, your telephone, and the internet? Are these present "in the background?" If so, is that a good idea?

Full Attention While Studying

While studying, it's very tempting to multitask by having electronic devices nearby, alerting you to text messages and updates on social media. Or perhaps you have the television on, or music playing, even if just for background noise. All of these options are tempting because they're more interesting than studying. You may think, "Well, if I have to study, why not make it less painful by mixing in music, and occasional communication with others? I have to take breaks sometime, so why not do so when something grabs my attention?"

To answer that question, all we need to do is consider the typical competition between top-down and bottom-up attention. Top-down attention required for studying is already at a disadvantage because it requires effort. Then, when you make attractive distractions readily available, you're ensuring that top-down attention will be interrupted (probably multiple times).

Consider this analogy: What if you had to take a medication for a serious illness? You have two options. The first one tastes badly but is highly effective and requires the fewest doses. The second option tastes considerably better, but it's not as effective, and even then it requires more time to get those weaker effects. Which makes more sense? Of course in this analogy the first medication is studying without distractions, whereas the second medication is studying with music, TV, and electronic devices.

As unappealing as it may sound at first, the most effective studying occurs in a distraction-free setting. In addition to electronic devices and mass media, other people can be a major distraction, even if they are not interacting with us. Our minds are inherently wired to find other people to be very interesting stimuli, so if we hear people talking, or see them doing something, it can be extremely difficult to resist paying attention to them.

You might be thinking, "I can't possibly study in a place without any other people, music, television, or electronic devices. How boring! And besides, I *know* I study best with some background noise, or my favorite music, or taking breaks to check my online accounts." Good try. It's true that you're probably *used to* studying that way, and that you have a great incentive to convince yourself that it's fine (or even best) to study with pleasant distractions. Unfortunately, none of that changes the reality of the link between undistracted attention and learning.

It's true that if we're used to having multiple things going on at once, focusing on only one thing feels strange, maybe even uncomfortable, and we might not be very good at it yet. Concentration (top-down attention) is a skill, and gets easier with practice. That's why I included a chapter on practicing mindfulness, as it leads to greater ability to concentrate whenever desired.

Because the overarching goal is to ensure that your study environment is distraction free, make sure you're not hungry or need to go to the bathroom. And, as long as we're mentioning food, resist temptations for sugary snacks and drinks (including yogurt, granola bars, and foods made primarily of flour, such as crackers). The sudden spike in blood sugar is energizing and satisfying, but the rapid crash that comes afterward produces sluggishness and a lack of focus.

For motivation to change your studying habits, recall the medication analogy. Because studying is not fun, why not spend the least amount of time possible doing it correctly? That way, when you're done studying, you can truly enjoy your remaining time, rather than spending that time in a watered-down form of studying. The ideal is 1) to have your own distraction-free study space, and 2) to schedule dedicated study sessions during which you do nothing else. Then, when you leave your study space, you're done, free to focus on other things.

In the chapter on motivation and self-discipline we'll cover how to increase the likelihood that you'll follow these good intentions. And, in the chapter on studying, you'll learn to be engaged enough during your study sessions that you won't need distractions or entertainment. Trust me.

Full Attention in Class

Sometimes in class you don't have control over whether a distraction occurs, yet every distraction costs you in terms of attention, and therefore learning. In one study, psychologists compared two sections of the same college course. In one section the instructor elicited the cooperation of a student whose phone was called at a precise point while the class watched a video. The student fumbled for her phone, acting embarrassed as she turned it off as quickly as possible. Of course the ringing was a distraction for the entire class, but nothing out of the ordinary.

The psychologists were interested in the extent to which students in each section of the course learned the material that was being covered at the point in the video when the phone rang. On the two exam questions covering that material, nearly 90% of the students who were not in the distracted class answered correctly, but only 60% of the students in the distracted class did! When the researchers examined the students' class notes, students in the class with the ringing phone were 40% less likely to have the information in their notes. Yikes!

You may not be able to control distractions in class, but you can make sure you don't cause any yourself. That means making sure all electronic devices are turned off, you don't have a full bladder or an empty stomach, and any unnecessary things have been removed from your line of vision. When someone else does something that distracts you, your goal is to redirect your attention back to the material as quickly as possible. It's very easy for thoughts to wander away once we're initially distracted.

Lulls in the Action

Other problems with maintaining attention in class occur because there isn't anything important or interesting going on. The instructor may be talking about something irrelevant, or answering a student's question about something that makes perfect sense to you. During such times, it's easy to mentally check out, and thoughts wander to non-class topics. One strategy researchers have found helpful for such times is simple doodling.

Apparently, engaging in mindless doodling helps occupy enough attention to keep from more completely disengaging from what's going on around you. The key is to not become too involved in the doodling, but simply use it as a way to keep your hands busy and your attention on hold while you continue to monitor what is being said. Keep the doodling simple, and on a separate piece of paper that you can put away (and eventually throw away). As you realize that the class is back to material of substance, quickly shift your full attention to that.

As strange as it may sound, several researchers have found that chewing gum helps maintain top-down attention and focus. Although it's not entirely clear why it works, it does seem to be important that the gum be sugarless (see the earlier comments about the effects of sugar) and of a quantity and firmness that requires some deliberate jaw movements to chew. Chewing it rhythmically (steadily) also seems to be important. This is a good tip with which to end the chapter, as it can be used both while studying and while paying attention in class.

Memory

Much that we call learning relies on memory. So, understanding and improving memory are keys to learning. First, psychologists have identified different types of memory. For our purposes here, though, we're only going to focus on distinctions important for improving learning.

Short-Term vs. Long-Term Memory

We know from experience that some memories last a long time whereas others are short-lived. Psychologists too distinguish between short-term and long-term memory, but the nature of each isn't what most people think. Long-term memories are those that last more than a minute. Sure, some long-term memories last a lifetime, but most last less than a day.

Short-term memories only last about 30-60 seconds—just long enough to work with the information involved before it fades if it's not important for later. The idea is that we need to be able to remember information longer than a few seconds, so that we can accomplish whatever we need to in the moment, but after that, the information may no longer be useful, so it makes sense that it quickly fades forever.

To illustrate, have you ever had a long conversation, yet when asked later what the two of you talked about, you have a difficult time remembering anything from the conversation? Short-term memory allowed you to remember things long enough to keep the conversation going, but if nothing noteworthy occurred, very few long-term memories were made. Later, you have a long-term memory that you had a conversation, but few details made it into your long-term memory.

Of course lots of information is remembered for longer than a minute, and it therefore must have been stored in long-term memory. Also, if something is important, it only takes an instant to form a long-term memory of it.

What does all this mean for learning? While in class or studying on your own, the material may make sense at the time (while it exists in your short-term memory), but if you don't form strong long-term memories of the material, it will be gone shortly after presented. Remember hindsight bias from the chapter on beliefs? Now we see how it, combined with the very limited life of short-term memories, leads to a lack of learning.

As we hold the new information in short-term memory, hindsight bias lulls us into thinking that, because we understand it, we sort of knew it all along, and so we'll certainly remember it in the future. As a result, we fail to form a long-term memory of the material, and come exam time, we're left in the dark. If you've ever felt as though you've understood well the material in a course as it was presented, but then did very poorly when tested on that material, you realize that short-term memories plus hindsight bias does not equal long-term memories (learning).

Remembering Material Long-Term

What can you do to try to ensure that you learn the material? The answer lies in understanding how our minds are wired to make long-term memories. What cues the mind to remember something? First, when something causes a strong emotional reaction we tend to automatically remember it (form a long-term memory). This little unwritten rule for when to form a memory makes sense from the standpoint of survival: It's probably ok to let go of information and events not related to negative or positive emotions. However, if we experienced strong emotions, they may have resulted from rewarding or dangerous conditions, and we should remember those so that we can seek or avoid them in the future.

Similarly, we are more likely to remember things that are out of the ordinary than we are things that simply blend in with the norm. So, when something is unexpected, it tends to grab our attention and is more likely to be remembered. We'll see a little later in this chapter how we can take advantage of that fact to memorize material.

Another way that we tend to naturally form long-term memories is when we have to use information, or engage in deep processing of it, especially more than once. Passively encountering information typically is not enough to trigger formation of long-term memories, but thinking about something deeply and using information signals the mind that the material may be useful for the future, so it's worth remembering.

Of course there is no guarantee that all information associated with strong emotional reactions, the unusual, deep processing, or practical use will automatically make it into memory, but it's much more likely than if the information was unemotional, routine, and unused. Once formed, long-term memories can then be strengthened through recall and repeated use, thereby extending their life-span.

Retrieving or Recalling Memories

So far we've been focused on memory formation. However, if a long-term memory is to be used, we have to be able to retrieve or recall the memory. Indeed, psychologists have found that memory formation and retrieval are two separate processes. We've all had the experience of *knowing* that we know something, but not being able to recall it at the moment we need to. With exams there is limited time for retrieval, so it's important that long-term memories of the course material are easy to recall.

There is no foolproof way to make sure you can recall particular information you have learned. Of course the stronger the memory for that material (how frequently it was recalled and used), the greater the likelihood of being able to recall it. Also, the likelihood of recall increases with the number of different cues associated with that memory. Think of cues as all the extra information

41

associated with that memory apart from the material itself. Mental material that has lots of other "things" associated with it will be easier to recall than material not associated with much else.

Remember when I described that having knowledge about a topic makes it easier to learn additional knowledge about that topic? I explained that the existing knowledge might be thought of as wire mesh ball making it easier for new information to connect to. Now we see one primary reason why this is true. By fitting the new material into a larger set of existing knowledge, the new bit has more associations to existing long-term memories, making it easier to recall. A rich network of knowledge not only makes it easier to understand and integrate new information, but it also provides more connections (cues) associated with that new material (boosting the likelihood of recall).

There's good news for those who need to learn about a topic but do not have much prior knowledge about it: lots of things can serve as memory cues. The setting in which we learned the material, how we felt at the time, what happened immediately before and after we learned the information, and much more all may serve as helpful retrieval cues. For example, memories formed in one location are easier to recall in that same location. So, students score higher on exams when tested in the same room in which class was held, because the room serves as a cue for memories of material presented in class.

Now we understand the difference between short-term and long-term memory, and the importance of capitalizing on ways our minds are most easily led to form long-term memories of new material. We also realize that just as important is trying to ensure that information, once learned, can be retrieved when needed.

With this basic understanding of memory, we will apply these principles in the chapters on studying and spending time in class. First, however, there is a set of well-established methods for ensuring that new material is firmly anchored to cues that already exist in long-term memory. Collectively, these methods are referred to as mnemonic techniques.

Mnemonic Techniques

If we need to learn something new, tying the new material to something already firmly in memory helps increase the likelihood of remembering the new material in the future. All we have to do is recall the earlier memories, which should prompt recall of the new material we associated with them.

If you were ever taught a new song (perhaps an educational one) sung to an old tune, you used a mnemonic technique for learning something new. Or, if you remember that daylight savings time involves "springing ahead in the spring" and "falling back in the fall," you've used a mnemonic to remember whether to set your clocks ahead or back.

Let's consider some particular mnemonic strategies for remembering information, and being able to recall it on demand.

Acronyms and Acrostics

Acronyms involve taking the first letter from each of a set of words and creating a new word with those letters. For example, in psychology there are five primary clusters of personality traits (known as "The Big 5") and each cluster has a name: Neuroticism, Agreeableness, Openness [to Experience], Conscientiousness, and Extroversion. Taking the first letter from each of these labels results in the acronym OCEAN. Because there is no order to the personality trait clusters, the first letters could be arranged in any way that makes a word that's easy to remember. What about when the order of the information is important?

Acrostics involve taking those first letters from the information to be learned and creating a sentence or phrase in which each of the words starts with the same letter. Now we just need to create a sentence or phrase that preserves the correct order of the information. For example, what if you needed to be able to recall the order of the planets from the sun? You might know the names of the planets, but remembering the order, and making sure you don't leave out any, is where an acronym or acrostic helps.

Taking the first letter of the name of each planet in order based on distance from the sun yields M-V-E-M-J-S-U-N. Because these letters do not naturally form a word, some students use the following sentence, with the first letter of each word representing the first letter of each planet:

My **V**ery **E**ducated **M**other **J**ust **S**erved **U**s **N**achos (or **N**oodles).

The Method of Loci (Location)

It's often easier to remember vivid images than verbal information. Some students take advantage of this fact by creating memorable images to represent material that needs to be learned. The issue then is how to remember what material was converted into images.

Chances are good that there are particular locations that are well-established in your memory—perhaps your childhood home, your current residence, or your favorite place to shop. For such locations, you carry around a mental map, which you can use to anchor new material in memory. Mentally "walk through" the location you select, and take your time depositing the bits of new information in separate places. The trick is to make sure the new material is vividly associated with each place within the mental map. The more unusual, even outrageous, the connection, the greater the likelihood you'll remember the information needed.

If two pieces of information are related to each other, you can represent that association by having the images wrapped around each other, or crashing into each other. If the nature of the association is important, such as whether two historical figures got along well or fought each other, include that in the image. So, perhaps the two figures are pictured passionately kissing (for liking each other) or boxing each other (for fighting). Remember, the more vivid and outrageous the image, the easier it is to remember.

As an example, let's assume that you need to remember Erik Erikson's eight stages of psychosocial development (something every psychology student has to learn at some point). Each of these stages involves a primary psychosocial dilemma that has to be resolved during that phase of development (so the order is important).

The first stage, during infancy, is Trust vs. Mistrust, and is associated with feeding. Assuming you're using a mental map of your childhood home, imagine walking through the front door. There you immediately encounter an infant, wearing only a diaper, standing alone in the corner looking very mistrustful. You try to hand him a full bottle, but he alternates between wanting to take the bottle from you and deciding not to because he's wary of whether to trust you. The more vividly you picture the infant's reactions, and expressions, the easier it will be to recall that Erikson's first stage of psychosocial development is Trust vs. Mistrust, and involves feeding.

The second stage of development is Autonomy vs. Shame and Doubt, and involves toilet training. As you walk into the next room in your childhood home, you see a toddler sitting on a potty chair, pants around his ankles. As the toddler stands up, you notice that the potty is full. The child looks to you with pride over having done this all by himself, but then looks away suddenly with shame over the fact that you've seen this "dirty" deed. Can you picture it?

Of course you would continue this process for all eight stages in Erikson's model of psychosocial development. Creating these mental images takes time and effort, but if done with full attention and with creation of vivid images, it will be nearly impossible to forget the information.

The Pegword Method

This technique requires first learning a list of objects, each corresponding to its own number in the list. It's important to memorize the particular object associated with the particular number. Once the list of objects is well-established in memory, then it's easy to associate new material you need to learn with individual objects in the list. To recall the new material, all you need to do is bring up in memory the object corresponding to that number. Before illustrating the process, here is the list of objects /numbers:

1 = Bun (perhaps a hotdog or sandwich bun)

2 = Shoe

3 = Tree

4 = Door

5 = Hive (bee hive)

6 = Sticks (perhaps a bundle of sticks, or long sticks stuck into the ground)

7 = Heaven (your vision of what heaven would look like)

8 = Gate (could be a simple wooden gate or a large iron gate)

9 = Wine (a bottle or poured glass of wine)

10 = Hen

11 = Kevin (hopefully you know someone named Kevin whom you can picture)

12 = Elf (one of Santa's helpers?)

13 = Curtain

14 = Fort (perhaps a wood or stone fort as you would see in a historical movie)

15 = Fife (a very small flute)

Notice that each object rhymes (at least somewhat) with the number it corresponds to, hopefully making it easier to learn or memorize. You might choose to start with the first 10, and add to your list later if you find the technique helpful. Beyond the first ten, it gets increasingly difficult to think of objects or people to rhyme with the number.

Once you've memorized the list to the point that you can easily recite it ("One is bun, two is shoe, three is tree ..."), learning new material involves picturing the interaction of the new material with the established items in the list. This technique is best for remembering concrete items but can be adapted in many ways depending on your creativity and imagination.

For our example, let's assume that you need to remember the Mohs scale for mineral hardness. There are 10 grades of hardness, each with a corresponding mineral (so it's important to remember the correct mineral for each number on the scale):

1 = Talc, 2 = Gypsum, 3 = Calcite,
4 = Fluorite, 5 = Apatite, 6 = Feldspar,
7 = Quartz , 8 = Topaz, 9 = Corundum,
10 = Diamond

In the pegword list, 1 = Bun, so close your eyes and picture a hotdog bun heaped full of white talcum powder. In the pegword list 2 = shoe, so close your eyes and picture a stereotypically dressed Gypsy woman dancing with huge shoes on her feet. Number 3 is trickier. In the pegword list 3 = tree. You could picture a large tree whose branches are loaded down with little cutouts in the shape of California. Of course "Cal" is only the first part of Calcite, so hopefully that would be enough to prompt the full word. Similarly, picturing a tree from whose branches hang milk cartons would work if it prompts you to think "calcium" as a reminder for Calcite.

The images you come up with in using the pegword method may seem ridiculous, but that's a good thing. The more outrageous the images the more easily you'll recall them. This method works best for people who can vividly imagine something, and it can take some creativity to come up with the images. For example, consider #5 on Mohs scale: Apatite. In the pegword list 5 = Hive, so perhaps imagining an ape hugging tightly (ape-tight) a beehive would do the trick.

Numbers for Letters

If you need to frequently remember strings of numbers, such as dates or constants for mathematical equations, it may be worth using the numbers-for-letters technique. For many people it's easier to remember verbal material than it is a date or a string of numbers, so converting the numbers into a word or phrase makes learning easier and more likely. Here is a proposed scheme to memorize to get started:

0 = **s** *or* **z** (note that spoken 0 starts with z)

1 = **t** (note that t looks similar to 1)

2 = **n** (note that n has two "legs")

3 = **m** (note that m has three "legs")

4 = **r** (note that spoken 4 ends in r)

5 = **f** *or* **ph** (spoken 5 starts with this sound)

6 = **sh** *or* **ch** (similar sounds)

7 = **k** *or* **g** (both "hard" sounds)

8 = **p** (8 and p have some visual similarity)

9 = **b** *or* **d** (9 upside down looks like b or d)

After the above list has been well-learned, memorizing a date or string of numbers involves translating each digit to its letter, and then creating a word or phrase from those letters (maintaining the correct order). Any letters used between the translation letters can be ignored when decoding (so it's important not to use any of the letters in the list unless they are part of what needs to be memorized).

Suppose that you have to remember the date associated with particular events in history. Let's say that the first important date is 1797. Now, to convert the date to the letters represented by the numbers:

1 = t   7 = k *or* g   9 = b *or* d   7 = k *or* g

Possible words or phrases from these letters (in order) include ta<u>k</u>e, ta<u>g</u>, and tu<u>g</u> for the first two numbers (1 and 7) and <u>b</u>a<u>g</u>, <u>b</u>ac<u>k</u>, <u>b</u>i<u>g</u>, <u>b</u>i<u>k</u>e, and <u>d</u>i<u>g</u> for the last two digits (9 and 7). If the date is for an important battle, you can close your eyes and picture both sides of the conflict facing each other at the battle front. Suddenly someone from the winning side runs over to the other side and "takes a bag" or "takes a bike" or "tags back" (choose one) and retreats to his own side. The important thing is to picture vividly the action associated with the phrase you choose to encode the date. Then, when you have to remember the date of the battle, you recall your image, which prompts the phrase, and then you can decode the date associated with the battle (1797).

Let's consider a second example: the date 1836. First, we convert the date to the letters represented by the numbers:

1 = t   8 = p   3 = m   6 = sh or ch

If we can construct a single word that uses all of the above letters together, in the correct order, that's great. Usually, though, it's easier to think of small words using those letters. So, the first two, t and p, can make top, or tip, or tap. The second pair of digits translates to such possibilities mash, mush, mesh, and much. Depending on what the date is associated with (a battle, death, or law?), you can choose the best combination of words to associate with it.

Admittedly, the letters-for-numbers method can take a good deal of effort and time depending on how easily the number in question translates into a word or phrase that makes sense and can be easily remembered (associated with the other information it relates to).

Oh, by the way, do you remember the example involving the first two of Erickson's eight stages of psychosocial development? Do you remember what the first two stages are? What about the example of the two sides at war in using letters for numbers? Do you remember the particular two-word phrase associated with that image? What about the first three minerals in Mohs scale of hardness (recall bun, shoe, tree)? If you remember any or all of these examples that you read casually as simply illustrations of the techniques, imagine how well you'll remember information you intentionally study using these techniques.

Michael W. Wiederman, PhD

Studying

We've covered what your environment should be like during study time (distraction free, including electronic devices and other people). In this chapter, we get down to studying itself. Let's start with answering this question: What do you currently do to study material from readings or class notes?

Several researchers have surveyed college students as to their study behavior. Across studies, the large majority of students report that their primary study method is review: they go over the material again and again, trying to reinforce it in memory. If the method is so popular, it must work, right? Fortunately, psychologists have tested various methods of studying, and the verdict is clear: reviewing material is one of the *least* effective methods for learning.

If reviewing is so ineffective, why do so many students rely on it for studying? Part of the problem is that most of us are not very good at being able to judge how well we know material we recently learned (or are trying to learn). Remember hindsight bias? While we review material, it is right there in front of us, and we've been thinking about it, so it feels as though we know it pretty well. As we go over the material again and again, it becomes increasingly familiar, and feels even more "known."

Now imagine sitting down in class on exam day. The instructor distributes the exam, and you're asked to remember the course material "from scratch" and in ways that allow you to answer the various questions posed by the instructor. Yikes! Now your mind goes blank, or you remember only fragmented bits and pieces. What happened?

Many students complain that they "studied hard and knew the material" yet "bombed the test." Unfortunately, these were probably cases of repeatedly reviewing the material but not actually having learned it, coupled with the feeling of assurance that comes from hindsight bias. Instead of rereading and reviewing, what should you be doing?

Hopefully, the overarching goal is deep understanding of the material, and how it relates to other things we know. As we encounter new material, in class or in a reading, we should focus on making sense of it in the context of what else we know. In other words, understand it, be able to explain it, apply it, and so forth. This is real learning, and knowing the material at this level means we won't be caught entirely unable to demonstrate our knowledge.

Tackling material with the goal of deep understanding is effortful, but it's also more interesting than passively reviewing it. When you fully engage with new material, the process should hold your full attention, even if the subject matter is not something that interests you that much. If you find your mind wandering, something is wrong. You may be too tired to study effectively, or you're not training your focus on the material. We've already covered some ways to boost top-down attention on the material, and more will come out as the book unfolds.

Assuming an adequate amount of attention, just how do you engage material in ways that keep you focused and prepare you for exams?

Studying *is* Retrieval

Fortunately, research has revealed the study technique that is clearly most effective: Retrieval. It seems that the mind is wired to initiate the process of laying down long-term memories of material it has to retrieve repeatedly. So, your studying should take advantage of this built-in tendency. Effective studying *is* retrieval of the material, even when your memory for the material is weak at first.

Because studying is retrieval, to prepare to study you need to generate quiz questions on the material you want to learn. To be both most efficient and effective, generate those questions at the time you're first engaged with the material. So, as you're reading assigned material, you should have paper nearby (or a word processing program open) and construct questions over each small chunk of material as you finish reading it. The same goes for notes from class.

The actual questions with which to practice retrieval depend on the nature of the course material and the types of knowledge desired. A math or physics course may require that you can solve new problems, whereas a history course may require that you can accurately describe and explain historical events. A psychology course may require that you can explain particular concepts and apply them to examples or new situations. So, the type of retrieval practice will vary and has to be adapted to each type of material (as well as what your particular teacher expects in terms of types of learning, as assessed on exams).

Good examples of question structures to use for engaging the material and achieving deep understanding include:

How are _____ and _____ different/alike?

Explain how/why _____.

How does _____ affect or relate to _____?

Why/how is _____ important?

What does _____ mean?

Describe a new example of _____.

What are advantages/disadvantages of ____?

What is the evidence for _____?

There are two reasons for constructing these questions at the same time you're reading. First, you are very familiar with the material immediately after you've read it. Hindsight bias leads to thinking you'll remember what you just read, but much (or all) of it will be forgotten. Second, the very act of thinking of an appropriate retrieval question will help prompt remembering the material (trust me at this point).

Perhaps students do not stumble upon this most effective method for studying because it involves an extra step at the point of reading. Rather than simply cruising along, passively reading paragraph after paragraph, it requires stopping along the way to think of and write out quiz questions, and that takes time and effort. However, this read-stop-write process prompts greater learning of the material at the time and makes effective studying much more time-efficient later.

Sometimes text books include self-quiz questions, and those might be a good place to start. Still, don't rely on those exclusively, as they're not necessarily complete. Plus, they weren't constructed with your particular course and teacher in mind. For math and other courses where the expectation is that you can solve new problems, retrieval studying consists of solving new practice problems. Do so to the point at which not only are you able to solve each type of problem correctly, but you understand how you did it.

Preparation for Retrieval

To save time, I recommend placing some notation after each quiz question you write, so that you can easily locate the correct answer later if needed. If the material is coming from a book, I'd note the page number, the column number (if each page has more than one column of text), and even the paragraph number. So, immediately after a quiz question, I might note 72-2-4, which means the answer is on page 72, in the second column, fourth paragraph down from the top. If the material is coming from class notes, I'd either number my pages of notes or number each major point or section in my notes, so that I could easily refer to where to find the answer for each self-generated question.

Some students prefer to write out the answer to each self-written question, rather than refer to where the answer is in the book or class notes. That's fine and works well, but it does take more time. If you go this route, be sure to jot down the answers in your own words (don't just copy it word-for-word from the text). The goal is to learn the material (which won't fail you) versus memorizing an answer.

Once you have your quiz questions and either the answers or notation on where the answers are, studying for exams now involves trying to answer each question. Even if you don't know the answer yet, simply try your best to come up with an answer *before* checking. The very act of trying to answer a question before looking up the answer helps prompt remembering the answer when you do then look it up.

How Long Should You Study?

How do you know when you're finished studying a set of material for a particular session? Answer: When you are able to successfully answer each question, you are finished. No, not forever. At this point, move on to other material, or take a break, or do something else.

What do I mean by "successfully answer" each quiz question? I mean being able to write out or verbally provide enough concrete information that you could fashion it into a high-quality answer if asked that question on an exam. So, it doesn't mean that you have to have a perfectly formulated and elegantly written answer, but there needs to be enough material to make clear that you understand and remember the answer. Do not rely on a sense that you know it, give yourself the benefit of the doubt with vague answers, and then jump to the next question. That's hindsight bias creeping in, and hindsight bias is not a friend on exam day.

Each time you study a particular set of material, include all the quiz questions for which the answer is not automatic and super-easy for you. In other words, even if you successfully answered a particular question last time, but there was any degree of hesitancy, include it each time you study that material until it becomes well-learned. Oh, and mix up the order of the questions, too. You don't want to learn to associate information (answers) only in the context of specific questions that came before or after.

If you don't have time to get through all questions in one session, that's fine. We'll learn later that smaller, spaced study sessions are better than less-frequent, massive ones. Study until you've successfully answered each question or you've run out of mental energy or time, whichever comes first.

One of the advantages of retrieval rather than simply reviewing material is that there is a definite end to a study session (when all quiz questions are answered correctly). In contrast, rereading and reviewing could continue indefinitely. With self-testing you gain the peace of mind that you really do know the material well enough to be tested on it. Then, you can enjoy the rest of your time free of guilt or worry (and take pride in your accomplishment).

Restoring Attention

Now you know how to study (practicing retrieval by answering quiz questions) and how long to study each time (ideally, until the point of mastery, or getting each question correct). Because this form of studying takes full attention, we now can appreciate the importance of having a distraction-free environment. Also, if you feel your attention lagging, take a break, stand up, stretch, walk around, chew sugarless gum, whatever it takes to be able to return to studying refreshed and engaged. If you have difficulty concentrating generally, the chapter on practicing mindfulness is for you.

Top-down attention requires mental energy that can become depleted as you "use it up." To restore this mental resource requires sleep or a period of quiet reflection. So, a growing body of research has demonstrated that spending a bit of time in nature, or even looking at images of nature, restores the ability to focus attention. Importantly, it's not just any leisure activity that has this ability, as watching television, socializing, or looking at images of cities does not improve attention.

Consolidate New Memories

What else can you do to ensure maximal learning? Well, forming new memories requires their consolidation in the brain. For that, resting and sleep are important ingredients. As popular as it seems to "pull an all-nighter" when studying for an important exam, missing out on sleep impairs learning and memory formation.

Ideally, students would get a good night's sleep every night, and especially prior to an exam. For that reason, I've included a special chapter on how to ensure you get good sleep. Still, you can (and should) build in memory-consolidating rest during study sessions.

Psychologists have experimentally compared learning with and without a period of mental rest immediately afterward. For example, in one research project two groups of students were asked to study the same material. Then, students in one group were asked to close their eyes and relax for 10 minutes (apparently thinking about whatever they wanted to think about), whereas the other group were asked to work on some word puzzles for those 10 minutes. The group who rested after learning outscored the other group when tested both immediately afterward and much later. So, try to end each of your study sessions with a bit of quiet, eyes-closed rest (or quality sleep if studying right before bedtime).

Recent research and theory have explained why we need breaks to mentally store what we've learned. If our attention is consumed with working on solving problems, storing what we learn during the process suffers. So, especially when working on math problems or other mentally challenging tasks, build in frequent little breaks to allow the larger lessons to be stored in memory.

How Often Should You Study?

When it comes to studying, a strong and consistent finding from research is that spaced studying is far superior to mass studying. In other words, breaking up study sessions on the same material is much more effective than spending the same total amount of study time in one cram session. Also, the longer the interval between study sessions, the longer we remember material.

As an example, suppose three students in a course each have 2 hours to devote to studying the same material for an exam. The first student studies in one 2-hour session right before the exam. The second student spaces out 2 one-hour sessions starting the day before the exam. The last student spaces out four 30-minute sessions during the week before the exam. Consistently, research has revealed that the second student will remember the material longer than the first student will, and the last student will remember the material longer than the other two students.

The effects of spaced studying are quite substantial. Enough studies have been conducted to be able to calculate the average effect. Across numerous studies, the average difference between spaced studying and one-shot studying is remembering 25% more material correctly! And remember, that's when the total amount of study time is the same for both comparison groups.

Warning: Realize that it's normal to start your second study session over a particular set of material and feel as though you're almost starting from scratch. That is, don't be surprised if you start the second session not doing well on being able to recall the correct answers to the quiz questions. Sometimes students feel discouraged and question whether it was worth spending the time and effort on the first study session. However, in terms of forming memories of the learned material, the first session did indeed have important effects. When reinforced with the second session, long-term recall of the material is greatly enhanced. Each step in the process is important, and it's not a one-shot method. Trust the strong science behind the recommendation of this strategy.

The spacing effect for studying has important implications for students faced with cumulative exams or a final exam that covers all of the material from the course. Spreading out the studying sessions during the term of the course will work best for being able to remember the material long-term (and isn't that the purpose of getting an education?). For this reason, students who take a course during a full-length academic term remember the course material longer than students who take the course over a condensed/accelerated term.

Going back to the example with the three hypothetical students, notice that, on the single exam, the student who crams right up to the exam may score almost as well as the student who spent the same amount of study time but spaced it out over multiple sessions. This possibility may explain why so many students seem to rely on cramming as their study strategy (it seems to work to a fair degree). The problem with cramming, however, is that the material learned for the exam is quickly forgotten, leaving the student with an exam score but not an education. If there is a cumulative quality to the material in the course or in the degree program, well, oops.

As the student who relies on cramming continues his or her formal education, learning remains difficult, like "starting over," because there is not as much of a cumulative effect. Recall that existing knowledge makes it easier to add new knowledge. Serious students space their studying time rather than waiting until the last minute. Because doing so requires planning and self-discipline, we'll tackle that issue in a separate chapter.

Study Buddies

What about a study partner for these self-testing sessions? Studying with another person is a double-edged sword, so consider the issue carefully before agreeing to it. On the positive side, being accountable to another person may boost motivation and make the process more interesting. Also, sometimes hearing what another student comes up with as good answers is beneficial, and characteristics of the study partner may serve as retrieval cues associated with the correct answer. So far, so good.

On the downside, there is always the risk that another person will distract from the activity that works (retrieval or testing each other). Too often, study partners end up being social partners. Having more than one other person present seems to increase the likelihood of distraction, without possible additional benefits. Be honest with yourself and ask whether you're considering a study session with others because it is the most efficient use of your time and energy, or because it sounds like it will be more interesting and fun (distracting).

Class

Always attend class. Yup, I'm being that absolute. In terms of being efficient, missing class handicaps you in multiple ways. Even if you obtain thorough notes from a classmate, you may not completely understand the material, and not even realize it, because the notes seem to make sense to you. The problem is that what you get from the notes and the meaning of the material presented in class may be two different things, and you may not find out until your exam answers on that material are scored as wrong.

Also, remember how we said that memories are easier to retrieve when they have multiple cues associated with them? Hearing and seeing the material in class are just such examples of important cues. The material has a richer context when experienced in class than when encountered only in notes or in a book.

We've already discussed the importance of avoiding distractions in class. One way to help lessen distraction is to sit up front. That way, the major point of focus is the instructor and any materials presented.

Many little things going on behind you won't even be on your radar, leaving you able to focus on what you need to learn. Also, being in front will create just enough self-conscious anxiety to keep you more engaged and paying attention than if you sat anonymously in the back of the room. It also doesn't hurt that the instructor gets used to seeing your face, as everyone tends to assume that dedicated students sit up front.

Of course there will be distractions grabbing your bottom-up attention, but you can do your best to refocus as quickly as possible using your top-down attention. In other words, when there is an unexpected noise or inappropriate comment or whatever, rather than letting your mind wander along thoughts related to the distraction, you have the power to refuse to go down that path. Simply stop. Remind yourself that your goal in spending time in class is to get what you need educationally, and indulging in distraction is the same as wasting your time and making excellence even more difficult.

Taking Notes

So, you're sitting in the front of class, engaged and avoiding distraction. What should you do with relevant material as it's presented or discussed? Always take the mindset that there will be a quiz or exam at the end of that class meeting. This mindset will prompt you ensure that you catch everything and understand it. Assume there is no tomorrow to study! So, if you hear or see something that doesn't make sense to you, stop the instructor at that point and ask for clarification. Recall that the curse of knowledge may be causing a blind spot in the instructor's view of what does and does not make sense to students.

Unfortunately, many students are reluctant to raise their hands in class because they fear they are the only one who doesn't understand what's going on, and they don't want to reveal their ignorance. In reality, most students may be feeling the same way and making the same assumptions. Still other students don't raise their hands because they aren't paying attention enough to realize that they don't understand. Do you want to sacrifice your education to conform?

He who asks is a fool for five minutes.
But he who does not ask remains a fool forever.

– Chinese saying

Now that you have the mindset that there will be a test at the end of each class, you'll be motivated to take good notes. "Good notes" means that they are accurate and complete enough that they will be useful to you when it is time to form self-testing questions and check your answers. Now that you have a clear sense of what your notes will be used for (generating self-testing questions and their answers), it should be easier to structure your notes to make sure they will be ready for the task.

Unfortunately, hindsight bias leads you to assume that the notes that make perfect sense immediately after presentation of the material will make just as much sense to you a week or two later. The solution is to include "too much" explanation in your notes. If it seems like too much at the time, it should be just right when you use your notes in the future. There may not be enough time to create detailed notes as the material is presented, but flesh out those details as soon as possible (such as during a lull in class, or immediately after class ends).

As much as possible, your notes should be in your own words, in ways that you would describe the information and explain the concepts to a friend. When instructors provide clear, plentiful notes in their presentations, it can be tempting to simply copy everything you see and hear. Usually, there's not enough time to do so, and the attempt will simply prompt anxiety as you fall behind. Even if you're able to keep up, copying can become a relatively mindless activity, and to focus on the details of the visual words, you have to tune out what is being said. You're liable to end up with a set of details without the larger context of understanding, and you may have missed some important points that were being explained along the way.

Remember that the goal is understanding, not having a set of notes in your instructor's words. Deciding what is important, and then translating into your own words is a powerful way to begin planting the material in memory. Plus, your notes will make more sense later because the descriptions and explanations are yours. If the instructor included one or more vivid or useful examples, briefly note those as well. Often such examples serve as great anchors for recalling what was going on in class when that material was being presented.

What about when a video is shown in class? Many students think of a video as a time to kick back and relax, and perhaps even be entertained. Sometimes that's the case—it depends on the instructor. Some instructors use videos to present new material, whereas other instructors use videos to provide examples and to reinforce material gone over in the text or in lecture. Unfortunately, some instructors do use videos as "filler" simply to use up class time when they have nothing else. Accordingly, it's wise to ask yourself why the instructor chose to show this particular video. Are there examples in it that relate to the course material? Are there explanations in the video that help clarify the material? What can you get from this video that will help *you* learn as much as you can and add to your notes?

Last, take advantage of small spans of unproductively used time. As long as you are sitting in class, why not take advantage of that fact for your own benefit? If you arrive before class starts, or finish class early, spend those few minutes making sure you have complete notes, discussing the material with a student nearby, creating self-quiz questions, or quizzing yourself. Learning during these little breaks means less of your free time spent studying. Plus, your studying is spaced out over time, a very good thing.

Motivation

All the knowledge in the world about how best to study will not make a difference if it doesn't translate into changing your behavior. Unfortunately, there is frequently a disconnect between what people know they should do and what they actually do. This chapter is all about using psychology to increase the likelihood that you won't be one of those people.

It's natural that coursework, assigned studying, and even attending particular classes is experienced as aversive. The activity is effortful yet often boring, or at least involves material you would not seek out if left to your own choices. Plus, when we're told to do something, our lack of a choice makes the activity less appealing. The problem with aversive tasks is that there are so many other activities that are preferable, even if only because they are *less* aversive.

When faced with a session of studying, it's very common to end up finding other things to do . "Um, I'm totally going to study right after I . . . um . . . organize my closet first." Sound familiar? Yielding to that temptation provides at least temporary relief from studying. In behavioral terms, the behavior of choosing some less-aversive activity over studying is reinforced or rewarded (even if the reward is the lesser of two aversive experiences). Behaviors that are reinforced are more likely to occur in the future. So, each time you avoid studying by choosing some other activity, you're even more likely to make such a choice in the future.

Because avoiding aversive experiences is a natural tendency, and is further reinforced every time you do so, it's important to take conscious control over your studying schedule. And, because studying is not naturally reinforcing (enjoyable), you have to provide other forms of reinforcement for engaging in the activity, especially at first.

Time

Let's start with scheduling. Without being explicit about *when* you're going to study, it's too easy to let other activities take priority. Ideally, you'd set a specific schedule for school work and study sessions, and that schedule would remain fairly consistent. If the non-academic aspects of life keep you from knowing far in advance when you can count on studying, then at least set specific times as far out as you can, even if it's just a couple of days ahead. This is important because it helps remove the spontaneous decision about whether you should study or do something else. The more you can make study sessions a routine, the more likely you'll follow through. The goal is to not have to think about whether it's time to study.

When scheduling homework and study time, remember that quality trumps quantity. The goal is to be efficient, getting the most done properly in the least amount of time. And remember, learning is effortful, so only schedule sessions for periods of the day when your energy and enthusiasm are greatest.

If you're a morning person, great; mornings are your best study times. If you're a night person, though, late mornings or afternoons are liable to be better than later in the evenings. Even if you don't find yourself getting sleepy in the evening, your mental energy and focus suffer from all the daily activities before that. Plus, evenings are frequently social and recreational times, and those temptations will be greatest then. At some level, students seem to know this, but have a difficult time following their own advice. For example, in a survey of more than 300 college students, more than 40%

believed that mornings or afternoons were the best times to study, yet 90% studied in the evenings or late night!

Assuming that you want a well-balanced life (not just school work), it's important to be efficient and take advantage of even small free periods during the mornings and afternoons. If a class is canceled or ends early, use that time to do school work. If you have an hour free between classes, hole up in a distraction-free study space and crank out what you need to do. Before going home, make it a routine that you squeeze in a set period of high-quality study time first. Think of the daytime as your work life (not social or leisure). If the daytime hours are well managed, you may be able to enjoy your evenings (at least many of them) work and guilt free.

Instead of controlling their schedules, it seems that many students let deadlines dictate what they work on when. So, if something is due the next day, or there is an exam the next morning, guess what they're doing while they should be getting valuable sleep the night before? This strategy is the opposite of spaced studying, so learning is short-lived. Also, what about busy periods where there are not enough hours in the night to get everything done? Trying to learn while tired and with little sleep is the least efficient approach. It's an example studying harder, not smarter.

I've heard students claim that they "work best under pressure," so that's why they wait until the last hours to study. Based on what you've read in this book, you know that can't be true. I suspect that such students have great difficulty with procrastination and managing their schedules. As a result, it's only when there is the pressure of a dangerously close deadline that they feel compelled to study, period. Now, however, you're too smart to fall for that trap. Plus, you want a life, right?

Regulate Rewards

Once you know *when* you're supposed to be studying, it's important to provide strong incentives to stick to the schedule. What activities do you value most? Watching particular television programs? Spending time with particular people? Enjoying a delicious treat? What else? *You* know best what is most important to you.

The tricky part is not letting yourself have the reward unless and until you've completed the scheduled studying. If you know in the back of your mind that you won't deprive yourself even if you fail to meet your goal, specifying rewards won't work. If you do stick to the plan, the reward provides an incentive to prompt the studying session, and when you get the reward afterward, studying is reinforced (making it more likely in the future). In other words, sticking to your studying schedule gets easier with practice.

The schedule-work-reinforce strategy is highly effective, but requires being the boss who withholds or bestows rewards based on your own behavior. Perhaps that's why we don't see as many people using it as probably should—it's difficult to punish yourself for not doing something you dreaded doing to begin with. If you don't think you can trust yourself to be the disciplinarian, it may help to enlist the help of friends to make you more accountable.

Secrets of Self-Discipline

What about those people who seem so self-disciplined that they follow through on their plans without needing an obvious incentive or reward? If you're not someone others would label "self-disciplined," these self-disciplined people might seem like mysterious aliens. Actually, it's no mystery; self-disciplined people are well-practiced at mentally rewarding (and perhaps punishing) themselves. Because it's happening inside their heads, we never see what's happening (and they may not even be aware of what they do to keep their own behavior in line).

Self-disciplined people typically feel anxious or guilty if they have something that needs to be done and they haven't started it yet. Anxiety and guilt are negative experiences (more so for some people), so there is an incentive to get started on the task. Then, the relief from the anxiety or guilt reinforces having jumped into the task that had been hanging over their heads.

Self-disciplined people also often reinforce themselves by thinking about what a good job they've done, or how good it feels to be done with the task, and so forth. Again, this internal self-talk may be so automatic that they really don't notice that it is a habit of theirs. So, it just seems like they "naturally" do what needs to be done.

I'm not saying that you have to become someone others would label as self-disciplined, but it is important to recognize that there is no mystery behind such people. The behavioral principles of reinforcement (reward) and punishment explain why some people seem more self-disciplined when it comes to studying. The moral of the story is simply that you must take control of the rewards and punishments for studying if you want to change your behavior.

There is no substitute for being very deliberate and concrete in the process of setting specific study times, determining the reward/incentive for completing that session, and then sticking to the consequences. It's also a good idea to pat yourself on the back and take well-deserved pride in your studying accomplishments. Reward each time you make the right choice, and not wait for a grade to be the reinforcement. In addition to this core strategy, there are some other things you can do to boost motivation and self-discipline. Let's look.

Employ Your Environment

Our environment tends to influence our behavior more than we typically recognize. So, if you want to help ensure that you follow your study schedule and maximize studying effectiveness, how might you alter your environment to tip the scales in that direction? What about simply making sure that your study schedule and class materials are clearly visible as a reminder?

What about setting one location as designated only for studying? If, for example, you choose an isolated corner of the library for your study spot, when you go there you know what you need to do. You're there for a purpose, and as long as you make sure there are no possible distractions present, such as electronic devices and other people, you can work most efficiently.

Shift Your Identity and Thinking

Next, it's important that you think of yourself as the type of student who studies regularly and takes personal growth and education seriously. A primary way to solidify this self-identity is to write out, by hand, your long-term educational goals and the changes you are making now to make sure you get there. It sounds hokey and therefore unnecessary. It's easy to dismiss the idea by saying, "I know that about myself. I don't need to write it out." However, research has demonstrated the importance of the act of writing it out (and keeping it) for lasting change. What do you have to lose?

Once you've written out your ideal image of yourself as a student, look for opportunities to share your vision with people in your life. Announce your newfound or renewed investment in your education, and what you intend to do to make sure you get the most out of your formal education (beyond just grades). Again, it sounds hokey, but the power of making commitments known to others is well established by research.

Although you value your long-term goals, it's natural to be more swayed by the temptation of small-but-immediate rewards over delayed ones that are larger. For example, imagine being asked, "Which is more important to you, an evening spent with friends or doing well on your next exam?" As a serious student, you might choose the exam performance. However, when faced with the actual choice between studying and having fun tonight with friends, well, you get the point. Fortunately, research has revealed a few ways to combat this natural tendency by altering your thinking.

The first way to resist the pull of short-term rewards over delayed ones is to make the later ones more vivid and concrete. Typically, long-term goals and their rewards seem vague. "Get into law school" is not as vivid and concrete as imagining a fun time when your friends urge you to go out with them. So, when faced with temptation, spend a few minutes imagining in greater detail what you want to accomplish, and the rewards for your hard work.

For example, if it's important to earn a high score on the next exam, imagine taking the exam and feeling well-prepared, answering each question with confidence. Imagine the instructor returning the exam and you see an A grade at the top. Imagine opening letters from impressive law schools, and discovering that you've been accepted. Imagine yourself as a successful lawyer. What would your clothing look like? What about your office? The more you can make your future as concrete as your present, the easier it will be to choose the behavior you need to make that future a reality.

Motivation and self-discipline are also bolstered by focusing on a higher level of abstraction. That is, rather than focusing on the immediate goal only, step back mentally and focus on the longer-range perspective. How does your behavior right now fit with that longer-range goal?

For example, imagine two students, each studying for the same exam. One is focused on getting the exam over with but earning a good grade. As a result, that student will likely study only as much as necessary to hope to earn a high score. The other student wants to earn a high score as well, but is focused on this exam as simply a step within a much larger process (ultimately the education is what's important). The results of research predict that the second student will be more motivated and patient during studying. Which student have you been? Which student would you like to be?

Another way researchers have found to boost self-control is by thinking about someone we know personally who has high self-control. So, when you find yourself having a difficult time getting down to school work, take a minute to think about someone you know who is a model student—someone who exhibits the greatest degree of self-discipline with school work. Then get to work yourself.

Last, there's a curious thing about humans: we tend to be more motivated to avoid losses than they are to score gains. So, when you feel your motivation waning, think about all of the time, effort, and money you have invested in your education. Skating by with the least amount of real, lasting learning is a waste of that investment. Focus on that perspective (losing what you've already invested) rather than on gaining a bit of fleeting free time by avoiding studying.

Other Tips

If you're not getting your school work completed despite maintaining a schedule, be sure to keep a log of your actual work. Tracking dates, times, and what you accomplished during each session will help make you more accountable and aware of what needs to change. You have to be honest with yourself, but often, seeing the cold truth prompts some improvement.

Faced with a large project or assignment? These can be overwhelming, prompting procrastination. "Study four chapters," or "write a 10-page paper," are intimidating goals. So, it's easy to come up with excuses such as there not being enough time to get started right now. Break large tasks down into definable steps and vow to accomplish just the first step right now. Reinforce yourself for doing so. Move on to step two. Repeat. Frequently, just getting started is the highest hurdle, and once we're over it, we're surprised at how much less intimidating the larger goal is now.

If you're really struggling to understand something, put it on hold briefly until you can ask for help. Between the instructor, teaching assistant or lab tutors, and classmates, someone should be able to help you "get it," thereby saving time and frustration. Of course move on to other work, in that course or in others, until you can get such help as soon as possible.

When you're at the point of quizzing yourself over the material, consider doing so while standing, pacing, or taking a walk. At the point where you no longer need to look up answers, all you need to carry with you are the questions. Constructing answers in your head while your body is more active should boost arousal and combat mental fatigue.

Last, you can take advantage of the motivational boost that comes from stimulating our bodily sensors that detect sugar. Research has revealed that stimulating those receptors wakes up the portions of our brain that drive motivation and the ability to focus in pursuit of a goal. The good news is that there are sugar receptors in the mouth as well as the gut, so you don't have to swallow the sugary drink to get the mental benefits. Besides the empty calories, recall that the problem with eating or drinking sugar while studying is that it impairs mental functioning after the initial rush wears off. Fortunately, simply swishing it around and spitting it out is effective. It does, however, have to contain actual sugar, rather than a calorie-free artificial sweetener, to stimulate the receptors and produce the motivational benefits.

People often say that motivation doesn't last. Well, neither does bathing—that's why we recommend it daily.

-- Zig Ziglar

Michael W. Wiederman, PhD

Recap

For this book to have any lasting impact on your learning, the strategies and skills described in it have to be practiced to the point of becoming second nature. Until then, a conscious effort is required to ensure you don't slip back into old ways. Habits have a persistent way of exerting themselves.

To make it easier to continue checking whether you're incorporating various pieces of the program, below is an outline of the specific approaches. Use it often.

Learning

Learn for Deeper Knowledge Rather Than Simply Grades (pp. 7-12)

Remember that Education is About Developing Skills and Abilities (pp. 12-14)

Beliefs

Work on Being an Incremental Theorist Rather than an Entity Theorist (pp. 15-18)

Assume You're Influenced by Hindsight Bias and Compensate Accordingly (pp. 19-20)

Assume Teachers Are Victims of the Curse of Expertise and Protect Yourself (pp. 20-23)

Realize that Learning is Effortful, and That Does Not Indicate Anything About Your Intelligence or Ability (pp. 23-24)

Consider the Importance of Deliberately Working on Weak Areas Rather than Only Strong Ones (p. 26)

Attention

Be Honest With Yourself About Multitasking and Resist the Temptation While Studying (pp. 28-33)

Avoid Sugary Snacks and Simple Carbohydrates While Studying and In Class (p. 32)

Avoid Distractions in Class (pp. 33-35)

Doodle During Lulls in Class (p. 35)

Consider Chewing Sugarless Gum to Boost Ability to Focus Attention (p. 36)

Memory

Know How Memory Works (pp. 37-43)

Use Mnemonic Techniques (pp. 44-55)

Acronyms & Acrostics (pp. 44-45)

Method of Loci (Location) (pp. 46-48)

The Pegword Method (pp. 48-52)

Letters for Numbers (pp. 52-55)

Studying

Study Using Self-Testing to the Point of Mastery During Each Session (pp. 59-66)

Restore Depleted Attention Through Time in or Looking at Nature (pp. 66-67)

Consolidate New Memories (p. 67-68)

Study Each Set of Material Multiple Times But Space Out Study Sessions (pp. 68-71)

Be Careful in Whether to Study with Others (p. 72)

Class

Always Attend Class (p. 73)

Maximize Attention and Focus (pp. 73-74)

Sit Up Front (p. 73)

Take Good Notes (pp. 74-78)

Keep the Mindset of an Impending Quiz at the End of Each Class Meeting (pp. 74-75)

Ask Questions & Request Clarification (p. 75)

Take Notes in Your Own Words, and Include Too Much Explanation (p. 76)

For Videos Ask Yourself About the Intended Purpose; Take Notes Accordingly (pp. 77-78)

Take Advantage of Small Spans of Time Throughout the School Day (p. 78)

Motivation

Set a Schedule for Studying, and Use Daylight Hours (pp. 80-82)

Build in Explicit Rewards for Meeting Each
Study Goal (pp. 83-84)

Move Toward Internalizing Rewards to
Develop Self-Discipline (pp. 84-86)

Alter the Environment to Encourage
Scheduled Study Sessions (pp. 86-87)

Write Out and Keep Your Goals for Yourself
as a Top-Performing Student (p. 87)

Make Your Goals Known to Others Who
Matter to You (p. 88)

Make Your Mental Images of Your Long-
Range Educational and Professional Goals
More Vivid (p. 88)

Focus on Larger, Long-Range Educational
and Self-Development Goals (pp. 88-90)

Think of Someone Who is a Role Model for
the Type of Student You Want to Be (p. 90)

Use the Pain of Loss for Motivation (p. 90)

Keep a Log of Actual Studying (p. 91)

Break Down Large Tasks and Assignments into Smaller Steps and Reward Completion of Each (p. 91)

Ask for Help Rather than Remaining Frustrated (p. 92)

Try Retrieval Studying While Being Physically Active (p. 92)

Stimulate Oral Sugar Receptors to Stimulate Motivational Focus (pp. 92-93)

In closing, this list is a reminder that you now have numerous proven strategies at your disposal. Use as many of them as you can and you will dramatically increase your learning effectiveness and efficiency.

With continued practice, these strategies will become second nature. By then hindsight bias will have led you to feel as though you've always practiced these methods and that this book was no big deal. I can live with that.

Let me know what worked and what didn't. I wish you all the best, in school and beyond.

Special Topic

Taming Test Anxiety

Anxiety and stress aren't necessarily bad, even when taking an exam. For example, researchers have found that the physiological arousal of anxiety can be useful when taking an exam that involves actively solving problems (rather than simply recalling information). Even when taking other kinds of tests, some anxiety is good for performance—it narrows your focus and provides motivation. It's only when anxiety becomes excessive that it tends to cause problems. Unfortunately, some students report a level of anxiety that seems to impair their ability to demonstrate their knowledge.

Sufferers of test anxiety report feeling overwhelmed by anxiety, so they have difficulty concentrating and remembering learned material. Some even experience full-blown panic attacks, making it virtually impossible to focus on the exam. Why do some people experience test anxiety and others do not?

There is no one answer. However, some people are simply more prone to anxiety in

101

general due to their physiological makeup. Such anxiety proneness tends to run in families, and is thought to result from differences in the brain's chemistry or sensitivity to anxiety-provoking situations.

Fortunately we live in a time in which we have safe, effective medications for treating the source of anxiety, rather than simply masking feelings. So, if you're a generally anxious person, realize that there is no need to let unusually high levels of anxiety interfere with your life. Because we're talking about tweaking brain chemistry, it's important to consult a qualified professional specializing in the brain: a psychiatrist.

A good psychiatrist not only has a lot of experience treating anxiety, but he or she is aware of the latest research and possible ways to effectively combine medications if necessary. Two people may have very similar symptoms, yet a medication that works well for one may not for the other.

Unfortunately, there is often a sense of stigma around consulting a psychiatrist. The result is that many people whose lives would be greatly improved by the medical advances that have been made over the last several years continue to suffer needlessly.

Rest assured that treating anxiety is a major focus of psychiatrists' daily work. And, because of the biological nature of general anxiety, patients are not psychoanalyzed. You're not liable to be asked questions about your childhood or your dreams.

In addition to a biological or genetic proneness to anxiety generally, what else contributes to test anxiety? One important factor seems to be how students perceive the testing situation, and the ways they think about what is occurring during the test.

For example, research on the effects of time pressure on test performance revealed that how students viewed the nature of the test questions made a large difference in terms of performance. When exam items were thought of as ways to gain points and demonstrate knowledge, time pressure had much less negative effect than when exam items were viewed as possible ways to lose points and reveal what students didn't know.

So, try your best to maintain such a "gains" perspective throughout the exam, especially as you feel pressure because class time is running out. Instead of thinking about how many unanswered questions you have, and the points lost if they remain unanswered, focus instead on how many items you've completed, and the points you've "banked" by at least having those items finished.

A general theme in the thoughts that cause test anxiety is the tendency to catastrophize, or jump to the worst conclusion possible. For some students, the catastrophizing starts even before the exam is distributed to the class. If the individual focuses on not being prepared enough, or imagines "drawing a blank" or panicking during the exam, the student understandably begins to feel anxious. Because test anxiety has been a problem in the past, the student now associates this flare up of anxious thoughts and feelings with the same bad outcomes as before, which causes even more anxiety.

Sometimes an anxious student starts the exam fine, but then something happens to trigger catastrophic thoughts. Perhaps the student does have difficulty remembering some key information needed, or the begins to focus on how little time remains. Once the catastrophic thoughts are triggered, the anxiety soars, further impairing the ability to focus on the exam at hand.

There are some practical things you can do to help ensure that catastrophic thoughts are not triggered. Of course being prepared for the exam by having effectively studied is a big one. Next, when you first receive the exam, skim over the entire thing. This will give you a sense for how long it might take, and which items are going to be most difficult or complex. Then, start with the easiest items first to build confidence and work up to the most challenging tasks.

The key is keeping anxiety in check before it grows. Negative thoughts and self-talk can act like gasoline thrown on a flame. So, it's important to learn to recognize such thoughts, and then take control of them. Based on your past experiences with test anxiety, what seem to be your specific triggers? Imagine yourself sitting in a packed classroom taking an exam. What runs through your head?

Recognizing and combatting troublesome thoughts is a skill, so it gets easier with practice. Ultimately you have to be able to pull the plug on those anxiety-fueling thoughts in the moment, during an exam, but you can start practicing while imagining yourself in a testing situation. Instead of running with the panicky thoughts, talk to yourself calmly and rationally with a soothing inner voice.

For example, suppose you draw a blank and can't remember the answer to the question you just read. A sure way to fuel the anxiety is to think, "Oh, no! I'm not going to get any points on this item. And what if I can't remember many of the other answers either? I'm going to fail this test!" Notice the catastrophizing. One moment of memory lapse quickly jumps to failing the exam.

A rational response to the example is to skip the item for now, telling yourself that you'll come back to it because there's no point in wasting time and stressing out over something you can't control. There may be something in subsequent exam items that prompts your memory for this item, or it may simply dawn on you later after the pressure is off. Even if it doesn't, there is nothing you can do to force a memory, and getting anxious is a good way to ensure that you don't remember this or other answers.

Some examples of rational self-talk that may come in handy during an exam include:

- "I'm doing my best, and worrying that it's not good enough doesn't help my performance or my health."

- "I'll do best if I stay calm and keep things in perspective. This exam is important, but it's not life-or-death."

- "Just because those students have already finished the exam does not mean I should be finished. This is not a race, and they may have turned it in because they left some items blank."

- "This exam is just one piece of the course grade, and even my performance on this exam does not necessarily reflect my intelligence or how much I've learned. Ultimately learning is the most important thing."

There are also some things you can do physically to short-circuit anxiety. For example, rhythmically chewing sugarless gum has been found to reduce anxiety and increase focus. Also, occasionally scan your body for signs of tension. When you find some, take a few seconds to stretch that body part and focus on letting go of the tension. For example, if you find yourself hunched over the exam, very rigid and tense in your neck and shoulders, it's worth taking a few seconds to rotate your shoulders and head and stretch those muscles. Then take a slow, deep breath and let go of the tension.

The reason it's important to make sure your muscles are not tense is because the mind picks up on feedback from the body as to what emotion is being experienced. So, if your body is tense with anxiety, your mind is liable to jump to those anxious thoughts. If your body is relaxed, it's much easier to keep your thoughts calm and rational.

A key to relaxation is breathing slowly and deeply. Because anxiety is associated with physiological arousal, we breathe much more quickly when anxious. These quick breaths are often shallow and originate in expanding the chest rather than the diaphragm at the bottom of our lungs. During an episode of panic we may need more oxygen than we receive from such shallow breathing, leading to a feeling of lightheadedness and panicky worry about not being able to breathe.

To ward off a panic attack, and to remain calm generally, it's important to maintain slower, deeper breathing originating from the diaphragm. Focus on drawing air in through your nose, intentionally pushing your belly out to do so. When your lungs are full, let the air naturally release, through either your nose or mouth. A few such deep breaths usually short-circuits the panic cycle. To make such breathing second-nature, practice numerous times each day, until you find that you breathe that way without consciously thinking to do so. Also, be sure to read the chapter on mindfulness.

The general theme of this chapter is that test anxiety can be managed by taking control of your thoughts, breathing, and bodily tension. That's all easier to do with practice, and with enough practice it all becomes the norm and you no longer have to think about it. In the meantime, it's probably a good idea to get to class early on exam days, and spend those few minutes focused on the strategies described here rather than continuing to cram and anxiously go over your notes one last time. Because you've been studying the most effective way, you'll be prepared to tackle the material. Now prepare to head off anxiety.

Michael W. Wiederman, PhD

Special Topic

Getting Good Sleep

Research continues to reveal numerous ways that sleep plays important roles in both our physical and emotional health. That alone should be incentive for maintaining a regular sleep schedule and being protective of the quality of your sleep. The reason for a special chapter on sleep, though, is because there are also important effects for learning and memory. Still, students frequently view sleep as a luxury that can be sacrificed to help juggle all the demands of waking life.

There is no magic number when it comes to the optimal amount of sleep. Each person differs in how much sleep is needed, and the quality of sleep matters at least as much as the quantity. Some people are awoken throughout the night and remain unaware of it. Perhaps the awakening was very brief, or being awakened did not get encoded into long-term memory before returning to sleep. Unfortunately, interrupted sleep is not as restful. If the length of your sleep seems adequate, but you're still foggy and unrested, perhaps something is interfering with your sleep quality.

Our sleep-wake schedule is regulated by a hormone, melatonin, released by our pineal gland (a pea-sized organ underneath the brain). It's melatonin that makes us sleepy, and it's released based on a daily cycle as well as in direct response to darkness.

Now, imagine the life of a typical student: bedtime may vary widely from night to night, and there are bright lights present right up until going to bed. As a result, we shouldn't be surprised that students often have difficulty getting to sleep, or problems waking up clear-headed and refreshed the next day. Regardless of how many hours spent in bed, the sleep quality may be low.

What can be done to help ensure a healthy sleep life? Ideally, you should follow a fairly consistent schedule. The most important part of that routine is probably the most difficult to stick to: getting up at the same time each day. If you're sleep deprived or end up staying up late, you naturally want to sleep later. The problem is that you're then liable to go to bed "late" the next night, and a vicious cycle is created in which you get tired later and want to sleep in later as well.

If you maintain the same wakeup time, and stay up late one night, you'll simply be that much more tired at your usual bedtime the next night. No problem. Of course you may be tempted to take a nap during the day. Unfortunately, naps lasting more than about 20 minutes or so are detrimental to good sleep at night. Also, even brief naps should not be too close to bedtime.

Caffeine and other stimulants increase alertness and interfere with sleep. So, it's important that stimulant drugs have cleared your system prior to bedtime. In general, people tend to overestimate how quickly the effects of caffeine wear off. Physicians refer to the "half-life" of a drug; that is, how long it takes, on average, for the drug to be at half its original dose in our bloodstream. However, the reported half-life of a drug is based on the average, because the half-life of the same drug varies from person to person, sometimes widely. Also, the presence of other drugs can influence the rate at which the caffeine is metabolized or broken down and excreted.

Assuming your body is typical in metabolizing caffeine, how long do you think it takes to get to half its potency? The answer: 5-6 hours. For heavy smokers it's 7-

9 hours. And, the half-life of caffeine for women taking oral contraceptives is a whopping 10-12 hours! So, coffee or energy drinks at midday could affect trying to fall asleep that night. Also, consider alcohol; it causes drowsiness, but interferes with the quality of sleep. So, although alcohol seems to help with sleep, it actually interferes with the healthful effects.

We've already learned that light interferes with sleep by inhibiting release of melatonin, and it turns out that it's mainly light in the blue portion of the spectrum that has this effect. Unfortunately, that is the type of light emitted by fluorescent bulbs and the screens of electronic devices such as laptops, tablets, cell phones, and e-readers. So, ideally you should build in a period of at least 30 minutes prior to bedtime during which lights are dimmed and you're not staring into electronic screens.

Apart from its effect on melatonin, light itself can keep you awake or wake you from sleep. Because light is sensed even through closed eyelids, it's important to make the bedroom as dark as possible. Nightlights and brightly illuminated alarm clocks could be interfering with your sleep without your awareness. If you can't rid the room of light, consider getting used to wearing a sleep mask over your eyes.

If you find yourself thinking too much when you're trying to fall asleep, the next chapter on practicing mindfulness is for you. Also, if you typically have difficulty falling asleep, or staying asleep, you might consider taking melatonin in tablet form.

Virtually every store that sells vitamins also sells melatonin. However, because in the United States it's sold as a dietary supplement, it's production is not regulated like that of medication. The result is a lack of assurance that the tablet contains an effective formulation of the hormone. Because the half-life of melatonin tablets is only about 45 minutes, taking one may help with falling asleep but not necessarily staying asleep. Although difficult to find, some brands include formulations that are time-released over several hours.

It's important for attention, memory, studying, and exam performance that you get a good night's sleep. As you can see, though, it's difficult to do that just occasionally, when it's "really important," if you haven't maintained a healthy sleep routine. The good news is that your physical health, emotional wellbeing, and academic performance will benefit from your conscientious protection of your routine. Sleep tight.

Special Topic

Mastering Mindfulness

Mindfulness means being fully aware of as much of your present experience as possible--your thoughts, feelings, and senses. It sounds easy, and at one level it is. However, if you've never actually practiced mindfulness, you'll be surprised at how difficult it can be not to get sidetracked.

To get a taste of mindfulness, try the traditional method of meditation practice. While alone, get into a comfortable position. The classic body posture is sitting upright on the floor, back straight, legs crisscrossed and palms facing up resting on the inner knees/thighs. This is the traditional position, but it's not mandatory.

Once you're comfortable, try closing your eyes or relaxing them to lazily gaze at a spot in front of you. Then, simply be aware of what you sense, feel, and think. The difficult part is to have awareness without latching onto a particular thought and running with it or trying to control it. We have a habit of thinking rather than simply being in the moment. This is where practice comes in—it gets easier over time. Many people find it best to focus on breathing, especially at first. Slowly draw air in through the nose and let it leave naturally through either your nose or mouth. Try focusing on simply observing your breathing, letting it happen as needed.

Within seconds you'll find yourself thinking something, anything. "This is stupid. What's the point of this? What was that noise? That reminds me . . ." Of course this is just one example of an endless string of possible mental chatter. It's this tendency to talk to ourselves that's the opposite of mindfulness.

Realize that thoughts will emerge, even as you try not to have any. Rather than trying to suppress your thoughts, let them emerge and settle as they will. Imagine a stream running through your head, filled with fish (thoughts) all swimming in the same direction. As one fish (thought) swims by there is probably another right behind it. Try to observe the flow rather than grabbing onto any one thought. As you catch yourself following a thought that popped up from the stream, simply let go of the thought (stop thinking about it) and go back to observing. It's common, at first, that you then think about how you grabbed onto that thought, and how difficult this is, and how poorly you're doing at it. Of course these too are thoughts, so let them go. Just observe.

Now you have a sense for how this simple activity--maintaining only awareness of the present--is not easy at first. Like anything that takes practice, though, it does get easier. Of course all this talk of difficulty and practice begs the question: What's so great about mindfulness? Why should I practice?

Over the past several years mindfulness has become a very popular topic with both researchers and practicing psychologists. There is now good evidence that practicing mindfulness benefits our physical, emotional, and mental health. For example, mindfulness reduces stress and provides all of the health benefits associated with stress reduction. Similarly, people who practice mindfulness tend to report less anxiety and depression. For our purposes here, though, the important point is that mindfulness is related to improvement in the ability to concentrate and avoid irrelevant thoughts.

Consider a study in which college students were randomly assigned to attend one of two classes; either on nutrition or mindfulness. Each class met for 45 minutes, four times per week for two weeks. In addition to

119

learning about and practicing mindfulness in class, students were asked to practice 10 minutes each day on their own. The nutrition students tracked their diets as homework. On a reading comprehension test taken both before and after the two weeks, the scores of students in the mindfulness class improved substantially, whereas the scores of students in the nutrition class did not. The students from the mindfulness class also reported fewer distracting thoughts during the test, and researchers suspect that was the key to their higher test scores.

The good news is that mindfulness can be cultivated outside of formal meditation. Simply practice being mindful of each activity you perform. Instead of thinking about other things while performing physical activities, pay full attention to what you're doing in the present. As you brush your teeth, focus on what you're doing, and how the process feels in your mouth. As you're driving or riding in a vehicle, pay attention to what you see and hear without getting distracted by thoughts that take your attention someplace else. The same for eating, or having conversations. As you practice, notice the benefits with regard to your mood and concentration. Enjoy.

Special Topic

For Female & Ethnic Minority Students

"When it comes to learning math, science, and technology, females just aren't as good at it compared to males."

"Everyone knows that _____ [fill in with just about any ethnic minority group] aren't very smart. If it weren't for special treatment, they wouldn't even have made it this far in school."

These statements reflect a couple of the most common stereotypes about how intelligence and school performance relate to gender and ethnicity. It's not that the stereotypes are true, but the fact that they are so common ends up causing problems for students from these stereotyped groups. How? Researchers have documented a phenomenon they label "stereotype threat."

If a particular stereotype is well-known, it lurks in the back of most peoples' minds. Then, when placed in a situation in which a person's behavior or performance might end

121

up reinforcing that stereotype, the individual from the stereotyped group may feel pressure not to prove the stereotype correct.

Imagine a young woman in an advanced math or science class with mostly male classmates. Although no one may talk about the stereotype explicitly, most everyone in the class knows about it, including the young woman. At some level, perhaps not even consciously, she recognizes that if she does poorly, she ends up providing "evidence" that females are inferior in math or science. Stereotype threat is this added form of pressure that males do not face.

Of course the same process applies to students from ethnic minority groups that traditionally have not scored as well on standardized tests, or graduated at similar rates as white students. Although there are explanations for these differences that have nothing to do with intelligence, stereotypes often imply some inherent inferiority of the minority group members. So, stereotype threat rears its head again.

Several lines of research have demonstrated that the added anxiety or pressure from stereotype threat impairs performance on exams. Even scarier, students experiencing such interfering stereotype threat were not aware of it. Might this apply to you?

Fortunately, research on stereotype threat has revealed a couple of simple-yet-effective strategies to combat its effects. The primary technique that has been studied involves values affirmation. Choose some aspect of yourself that is important to you. In other words, think of something about yourself of which you're proud. Is it your honesty, your compassion for other people, or perhaps a particular talent or ability?

Next, simply write a little about why that quality is important to you, and how it brings you closer to other people. How does this quality help with making friends and being well liked?

Importantly, this little exercise has been shown to erase the effects of stereotype threat on exam scores. Although researchers have only tested actual writing about the personal quality, if you find yourself short on time, at least spend a few minutes prior to the exam thinking through the prompts and your answers to them.

In addition to values affirmation, some researchers have tested the effects of changing stereotyped students' mental approach to the exam (specifically, the level of abstraction of the goal). Rather than thinking of the exam as simply a means to earning a grade, think of the exam as a way to build and practice skills. In research, those stereotyped students who emphasized learning over grades outscored the other students, presumably because the shift in focus reduced stereotype threat. Note that the shift in focus was prompted immediately prior to the exam, so the positive effects on exam scores were not due to extra studying or preparation.

The moral of the story is that if you are a member of a group about which there are stereotypes, you may be unknowingly influenced by those stereotypes, even if you yourself don't believe them. Simply feeling pressure to make sure your performance doesn't end up confirming the stereotype is enough to interfere with your concentration, memory, and test performance.

Fortunately, the strategies proven to combat stereotype threat are both simple and powerful. They certainly can't hurt, and sound research indicates that your exam scores will better reflect your actual knowledge rather than the effects of anxiety.

Reference Notes

Page 5: ". . . surveys have revealed that the large majority of students rely on study techniques that researchers have found to be . . . least effective."

Hartwig, M.K., & Dunlosky, J. (2012). Study Strategies of College Students: Are Self-Testing and Scheduling Related to Achievement? *Psychonomic Bulletin and Review*, Vol. 19, pp. 126-134.

Page 10: "Psychologists have tested the various shortcuts touted over the years . . ."

50 Great Myths of Popular Psychology: Shattering Widespread Misconceptions about Human Behavior, by S.O. Lilienfeld, S.J. Lynn, J. Ruscio, & B.L. Beyerstein (Blackwell Publishing, 2010).

Page 10: " . . . a network of established knowledge makes it easier to learn new information."

A good explanation of the science behind this fact is presented in the book *Why Don't Students Like School? A Cognitive Scientist Answers Questions About How the Mind Works and What It Means for the Classroom*, by Daniel T. Willingham (San Francisco: Jossey-Bass, 2009).

Page 17: ". . . Incremental Theorists are more likely than Entity Theorists to persist in studying . . ."

Carol Dweck is the psychologist who conducted pioneering work on how our beliefs about our own abilities shape our behavior. She summarized this work for a lay audience in her book *Mindset: The New*

Psychology of Success (New York: Random House, 2006).

A good example of promoting Incremental Theory with students to improve academic performance:

Blackwell, L.S., Trzesniewski, K.H., & Dweck, C.S. (2007). Implicit Theories of Intelligence Predict Achievement Across an Adolescent Transition: A Longitudinal Study and an Intervention. *Child Development*, Vol. 78, pp. 246-263.

Page 19: Hindsight Bias

This is such a well-established phenomenon that Wikipedia provides a good summary, along with application to various aspects of life: http://en.wikipedia.org/wiki/Hindsight_bias

Page 20: Teachers and the Curse of Expertise

The classic research demonstrating that expertise distorts views of how beginners will perform:

Hinds, P.J. (1999). The Curse of Expertise: The Effects of Expertise and Debiasing Methods of Predictions of Novice Performance. *Journal of Experimental Psychology: Applied*, Vol. 5, pp. 205-221.

Also, a thorough discussion of how topical experts (such as teachers) think qualitatively differently from beginners (such as students) is presented in the book *Why Don't Students Like School? A Cognitive Scientist Answers Questions About How the Mind Works and What It Means for the Classroom*, by Daniel T. Willingham (San Francisco: Jossey-Bass, 2009).

Page 25: "In a book on the 50 greatest myths of popular psychology, learning styles made the list."

The fascinating book is *50 Great Myths of Popular Psychology: Shattering Widespread Misconceptions about Human Behavior*, by S.O. Lilienfeld, S.J. Lynn, J. Ruscio, & B.L. Beyerstein (Blackwell Publishing, 2010). The direct quote is from p. 96.

A very readable review on learning styles that comes to the same conclusions is in the book *Why Don't Students Like School? A Cognitive Scientist Answers Questions About How the Mind Works and What It Means for the Classroom*, by Daniel T. Willingham (San Francisco: Jossey-Bass, 2009).

A scholarly review of the research on learning styles comes to the same negative conclusions: Pashler, H., McDaniel, M., Rohrer, D., & Bjork, R. (2008). Learning Styles: Concepts and Evidence. *Psychological Science in the Public Interest*, Vol. 9, pp. 105-119.

Page 25: "Research has shown that using a greater range of different types of teaching to cover the same material is most effective generally."

For example: Massa, L.J., & Mayer, R.E. (2006). Testing the ATI Hypothesis: Should Multimedia instruction Accommodate Verbalizer-Visualizer Cognitive Style? *Learning and Individual Differences*, Vol. 16, pp. 321–336.

Page 28: "Psychologists have found that multitasking often involves rapidly shifting attention or focus between two or more tasks."

Psychologists have studied multitasking since at least the 1930s, but here is a recent review article:

Altmann, E.M., & Gray, W.D. (2008). An integrated model of cognitive control in task switching. *Psychological Review*, Vol. 115, pp. 602–639.

Page 29: "One problem with multitasking is that it uses more of our mental reserves, depleting them sooner than concentrating on one thing. "

Kaplan, S., & Berman, M.G. (2010). Directed Attention as a Common Resource for Executive Functioning and Self-Regulation. *Perspectives on Psychological Science*, Vol. 5, pp. 43-57.

Page 33: "In one study, psychologists compared two sections of the same college course."

End, C.M., Worthman, S., Mathews, M.B., & Wetterau, K. (2010). Costly Cell Phones: The Impact of Cell Phone Rings on Academic Performance. *Teaching of Psychology*, Vol. 37, pp. 55-57.

Page 35: "One strategy researchers have found helpful for such times is simple doodling."

Andrade, J. (2010). What Does Doodling Do? *Applied Cognitive Psychology*, Vol. 24, pp. 100-106.

Page 36: ". . . researchers have found that chewing gum helps maintain . . . focus."

There have been more than a dozen studies showing mental benefits to chewing gum. Here is a site that reviews the research for the public:

http://scienceblogs.com/developingintelligence/2009/0
7/28/chew-on-this-how-mastication-e/

Page 57: ". . . the large majority of students report that
their primary study method is review . . ."

Hartwig, M.K., & Dunlosky, J. (2012). Study Strategies of
College Students: Are Self-Testing and Scheduling
Related to Achievement? *Psychonomic Bulletin and
Review*, Vol. 19, pp. 126-134.

Page 57: ". . . reviewing material is one of the *least*
effective methods . . ."

Dunlosky, J., Rawson, K.A., Marsh, E.J., Nathan, M.J., &
Willingham, D.T. (2013). Improving Students' Learning
with Effective Learning Techniques: Promising
Directions from Cognitive and Educational Psychology.
Psychological Science in the Public Interest, Vol. 14, pp.
4-58.

Page 59: ". . . research has revealed the study
technique that is most effective: retrieval."

The "testing effect" has been well-researched, and here
is a comprehensive review of that literature:

Dunlosky, J., Rawson, K.A., Marsh, E.J., Nathan, M.J., &
Willingham, D.T. (2013). Improving Students' Learning
with Effective Learning Techniques: Promising
Directions from Cognitive and Educational Psychology.
Psychological Science in the Public Interest, Vol. 14, pp.
4-58.

Page 59: ". . . the mind is wired to initiate the process of laying down long-term memories of material it has to retrieve repeatedly."

This exciting research uncovered what is happening throughout the brain that is different from what happens during other forms of studying:

Keresztes, A., Kaiser, D., Kovacs, G., & Racsmany, M. (2013). Testing Promotes Long-Term Learning via Stabilizing Activation Patterns in a Large Network of Brain Areas. *Cerebral Cortex*, Vol. 23.

Page 67: " . . . growing body of research has demonstrated that spending a bit of time in nature, or even looking at images of nature, restores the ability to focus attention."

Kaplan, S., & Berman, M.G. (2010). Directed Attention as a Common Resource for Executive Functioning and Self-Regulation. *Perspectives on Psychological Science*, Vol. 5, pp. 43-57.

Page 67: ". . . missing out on sleep impairs learning and memory formation."

Walker, M. P., & Stickgold, R. (2006). Sleep, memory, and plasticity. *Annual Review of Psychology*, Vol. 57, pp. 139 –166.

Page 67: "Psychologists have experimentally compared learning with and without a period of mental rest immediately afterward."

Dewar, M., Alber, J., Butler, C., Cowan, N., & Salla, S.D. (2012). Brief Wakeful Resting Boosts New Memories

Over the Long Term. *Psychological Science*, Vol. 23, pp. 955-960.

Page 68: "Recent research and theory has explained why we need breaks to mentally store what we've learned."

Barrouillet, P., & Camos, V. (2012). As Time Goes By: Temporal Constraints in Working Memory. *Current Directions in Psychological Science*, Vol. 21, pp. 413-419.

Page 69: ". . . the longer the interval between study sessions, the longer we remember material . . ."

This is a very old and robust finding in psychological research. One thorough review of the research is:

Delaney, P F., Verkoeijen, P.P.J.L., & Spirgel, A. (2010). Spacing and the Testing Effects: A Deeply Critical, Lengthy, and at Times Discursive Review of the Literature. *Psychology of Learning and Motivation*, Vol. 53,pp. 63–147.

Page 69: "Across numerous studies, the average difference between spaced studying and one-shot studying is remembering 25% more material . . ."

Cepeda, N.J., Pashler, H., Vul, E., Wixted, J.T., & Rohrer, D. (2006). Distributed practice in verbal recall tasks: A review and quantitative synthesis. *Psychological Bulletin*, Vol. 132, pp. 354–380.

Page 81: ". . . in a survey of more than 300 college students . . ."

Hartwig, M.K., & Dunlosky, J. (2012). Study Strategies of College Students: Are Self-Testing and Scheduling Related to Achievement? *Psychonomic Bulletin and Review*, Vol. 19, pp. 126-134.

Page 86: "Our environment tends to influence our behavior more than we typically recognize. "

Of course this is a generalization that can be applied in many ways. One such area containing lots of relevant research is on priming. Subtle cues in the environment may not catch peoples' conscious attention, yet they prime particular behaviors and responses.

Page 87: ". . . research has demonstrated the importance of the act of writing it out (and keeping it) for lasting change."

Getting people to stake out a particular position on a topic and commit to it by writing about it is a well-established method of persuasion. A recent bit of research along those lines, which also showed the importance of keeping the written statement compared to throwing it away is:

Brinol, P., Gasco, M., Petty, R. E., & Horcajo, J. (2013). Treating thoughts as material objects can increase or decrease their impact on evaluation. *Psychological Science, Vol. 24*, pp. 41-47.

Page 88: ". . . the power of making commitments known to others is well-established by research."

The internal pressure to be consistent with what we've proclaimed is a well-established psychological phenomenon. There's an excellent discussion of it in

Robert Cialdini's book *Influence: The Psychology of Persuasion* (New York: Harper Business, 2006).

Page 88: "The first way to resist the pull of short-term rewards over delayed ones is to make the later ones more vivid and concrete."

Psychologists refer to the tendency to take a smaller immediate reward over a larger delayed one "temporal discounting." Numerous researchers have examined factors affecting temporal discounting. Just one relevant example:

Kim, H., Schnall, S., & White, M.P. (2013). Similar Psychological Distance Reduces Temporal Discounting. *Personality and Social Psychology Bulletin*, Vol. 39, pp. 1005-1016.

Page 89: "Motivation and self-discipline are also bolstered by focusing on a higher level of abstraction."

Just one example of research that shows this effect: Fujita, K., & Han, H.A. (2009). Moving Beyond Deliberative Control of Impulses: The Effect of Construal Levels on Evaluative Associations in Self-Control Conflicts. *Psychological Science*, Vol. 20, pp. 799-804.

Page 90: "Another way researchers have found to boost self-control is by thinking about someone we know personally who has high self-control."

vanDellen, M.R., & Hoyle, R.H. (2010). Regulatory Accessibility and Social Influences on State Self-Control. *Personality and Social Psychology Bulletin*, Vol. 36, pp. 251-263.

Page 90: ". . . we tend to be more motivated to avoid losses than . . . to score gains."

This is a well-established finding referred to as "loss aversion." As such, the Wikipedia entry on that term is quite informative at reviewing the research and applications of the concept: http://en.wikipedia.org/wiki/Loss_aversion

Page 92: "Research revealed that stimulating those receptors wakes up the portions of our brain that drive motivation . . ."

There is an ongoing line of research on the role of glucose in motivation. Here is one relevant reference for the assertion made in the text:

Hagger, M.S., & Chatzisarantis, N.L.D. (2013). The Sweet Taste of Success: The Presence of Glucose in the Oral Cavity Moderates the Depletion of Self-Control Resources. *Personality and Social Psychology Bulletin*, Vol. 39, pp. 28-42.

Page 101: ". . . researchers have found that anxiety can be useful when taking an exam that involves actively solving problems . . ."

Jamieson, J.P., Mendes, W.B., & Nock, M.K. (2013). Improving Acute Stress Response: The Power of Reappraisal. *Current Directions in Psychological Science*, Vol. 22, pp. 51-56.

Page 103: "research on the effects of time pressure on test performance revealed that how the students viewed the nature of the test questions made a large difference . . ."

Roskes, M., Elliot, A.J., Nijstad, B.A., & De Dreu, C.K.W. (2013). Time Pressure Undermines Performance More Under Avoidance than Approach Motivation. *Personality and Social Psychology Bulletin*, Vol. 39, pp. 803-813.

Page 107: ". . . rhythmically chewing gum has been found to reduce anxiety and increase focus."

Sasaki-Otomaro, A., et al. (2011). Effect of Regular Gum Chewing on Levels of Anxiety, Mood, and Fatigue in Healthy Young Adults. *Clinical Practice & Epidemiology in Mental Health*, Vol. 7, pp. 133-139.

Page 111: "The reason for a chapter on sleep . . . because there are . . . effects for learning and memory."

Walker, M. P., & Stickgold, R. (2006). Sleep, memory, and plasticity. *Annual Review of Psychology*, Vol. 57, pp. 139 –166.

Also, the information in this chapter on sleep is fairly basic and can be verified by any reputable source providing an overview of the science of sleep. For example: http://en.wikipedia.org/wiki/Sleep

Page 119: ". . . college students were randomly assigned to attend one of two classes; either on nutrition or mindfulness."

Mrazek, M.D., Franklin, M.S., Phillips, D.T., Baird, B., & Schooler, J.W. (2013). Mindfulness Training Improves Working Memory Capacity and GRE Performance While Reducing Mind Wandering. *Psychological Science*, Vol. 24, pp. 776-781.

Page 121: Stereotype Threat or Identity Threat

There is a growing research literature on stereotype threat and how it affects academic performance. This article provides a summary of the research up to the point it was written:

Walton, G.M., & Spence, S.J. (2009). Latent Ability: Grades and Test Scores Systematically Underestimate the Intellectual Ability of Negatively Stereotyped Students. *Psychological Science*, Vol. 20, pp. 1132-1139.

Page 123: ". . . research on stereotype threat has revealed a couple of simple-yet-effective strategies to combat its effects."

A good example of research using the values affirmation strategy:

Schnabel, N., Pudie-Vaughns, V., Cook, J.E., Garcia, J., & Cohen, G.L. (2013). Demystifying Values-Affirmation Interventions: Writing About Social Belonging is a Key to Buffering Against Identity Threat. *Personality and Social Psychology Bulletin,* Vol. 39, pp. 663-676.

A good example of research using the mental level of abstraction strategy:

Stout, J.G., & Dasgupta, N. (2013). Mastering One's Destiny: Mastery Goals Promote Challenge and Success Despite Social Identity Threat. *Personality and Social Psychology Bulletin*, Vol. 39, pp. 748-762.

ABOUT THE AUTHOR

Michael Wiederman is a professor of psychology at Columbia College, a small women's college in Columbia, SC. He teaches introductory psychology, as well as a variety of courses on personality, disorders, counseling, and sexuality.

Dr. Wiederman has published more than 200 articles and book chapters, wrote the book *Understanding Sexuality Research*, and co-edited the *Handbook for Conducting Research on Human Sexuality*. He also is one of the handful of contributors answering reader questions at the popular site "Ask the Psychologist" (www.AskthePsych.com). He also can be found at his own site: www.MindingtheMind.com.

31991838R00080

Made in the USA
Charleston, SC
04 August 2014